ROMAN
LINCOLN

Conquest, Colony & Capital

ROMAN LINCOLN

Conquest, Colony & Capital

MICHAEL J. JONES

TEMPUS

First published 2002

PUBLISHED IN THE UNITED KINGDOM BY:
Tempus Publishing Ltd
The Mill, Brimscombe Port
Stroud, Gloucestershire GL5 2QG
www.tempus-publishing.com

PUBLISHED IN THE UNITED STATES OF AMERICA BY:
Tempus Publishing Inc.
2A Cumberland Street
Charleston, SC 29401
www.tempuspublishing.com

British Library Cataloguing in Publication Data.
A catalogue record for this book is available from the British Library.

ISBN 0 7524 1455 0

Typesetting and origination by Tempus Publishing.
PRINTED AND BOUND IN GREAT BRITAIN.

Contents

Acknowledgements

This book is partly the result of my close involvement in Lincoln's archaeology over a period of more than thirty years. During that time I have attempted to synthesise existing knowledge on particular aspects of the city's Roman past, but never before the whole of that period. An opportunity to produce an academic synthesis of the complete archaeological sequence of Lincoln, covering the archaeology of the city up to the industrial period, has been facilitated by the existence of an Urban Archaeological Database, together with the Lincoln Post-Excavation Programme, both largely funded by English Heritage. The preparation of this document, the Lincoln Archaeological Research Assessment (LARA), has been co-ordinated by David Stocker, who has edited a draft written by Alan Vince and the present author, and suggested a number of changes and improvements, as well as himself producing detailed Research Agenda for each era. The revisions have incorporated some significant changes and improvements, none more so than to the section on Prehistory, which is radically different from the original. The LARA will be a more substantial and fully-referenced document than this book. It is due to be published in 2003.

Both Dr Simon Esmonde Cleary (University of Birmingham) and Dr J.P. Wild (University of Manchester) have generously read a draft of the text of chapters 1-13 of the present work, and made a number of suggestions for improvements. Individual sections have benefited from the comments of others; they include Dr J.A. Johnston (chapter 1) and James Rackham (chapter 2). Professor Alan Straw kindly made available a copy of his latest thinking on the Lincoln gap.

For line drawings, I am grateful to the skills of former colleagues Helen Palmer-Brown, Jane Peacock, Tig Sutton and David Watt; the latter has prepared some new illustrations especially for this volume: **10**, **68** and **86**. Some others are taken from existing publications: **6** is reproduced from *Geology Today*, Volume 18, 2002, with kind permission of Professor Alan Straw; **11** and **12** by kind permission of Professor Malcolm Todd; **25** and **60** (this one based on the work of Ben Whitwell) by permission of Nicholas Bennett and Stewart Bennett, editors of the volume *An Historic Atlas of Lincolnshire* (1993, reprinted 2001); **27** was developed by Ben Whitwell from an article in *The Gentlemen's Magazine*, 1852; **32** and **34** are reproduced with the permission of the Society of Antiquaries of London; **41** and **42** are the work of the late Dennis Petch, who had passed them on to me in the hope that an outlet might be found for the publication of his report on the public baths; **46** is the work of Nicholas Reynolds, who also took the photograph which appears as **73**; **15** was taken from *Fortress into City* (edited by Graham Webster, Batsford, 1988). Figures **22** and **81** are based on the work of Jen Mann, and **82** on that of Margaret Darling and

Barbara Precious. The reconstruction drawings (**8**, **17**, **21**, **29**, **31**, **40**, **51**, **62**, **72** & **77**) are merely a sample of the output of David Vale, who did so much to bring ancient Lincoln to life.

Some of the photographs were taken by former members of the staff of the Lincoln Archaeological Trust and its successor Unit, including Christina Colyer, Nicholas Hawley and Kevin Camidge. For others, I am particularly grateful to Lincolnshire County Council (City and County Museum) for **3**, **4**, **14**, **35**, **47**, **48**, **61**, **64**, **65**, **75** and **80**, **colour plates** **1**, **6**, **8**, **12**, **14**, **19**, **20**, **21**, **25**, **26**, **27** and for the cover illustration; Lincolnshire Archives Office for **1** and **colour plate 9**; and the County Council's Tourism Section for **colour plate 28**. Figure **24** and **colour plates 2**, **3**, **4** and **29** are reproduced with the permission of the Trustees of the British Museum. Figure **66** was produced at the Environmental Archaeology Unit at the University of York, and **5** is the copyright of the *Lincolnshire Echo*. **Colour plate 5** is a photograph of a replica of the original and was taken by Peter Washbourn, who kindly allowed me to use it here. Figure **23** is the copyright of the Römische-Germanische Museum, Mainz. **Colour plate 10** is shown here with the permission of the Musée d'Aquitaine, Bordeaux.

The book has been written while I serve as City Archaeologist to the City of Lincoln Council, but in my spare time and periods of annual leave. The excellent library facilities of Bishop Grosseteste College, Lincoln, and of the University of Nottingham, where I am pleased to hold posts as a Part-time Lecturer and a Special Lecturer respectively, helped me make progress on many weekends and at other periods. My wife and family have again had to tolerate my physical absence and intellectual distraction over several months, time that should have been spent with them.

Peter Kemmis Betty invited me to write this book, and has shown great understanding while waiting for me to be free enough of other commitments to bring it to a conclusion. Emma Parkin at Tempus Publishing coped admirably with the task of preparing it for production.

Preface

I vividly remember my first encounter with Roman Lincoln in the summer of 1970. Still a research student at Manchester University studying Roman Fortifications, I had been offered, and keenly grasped, an opportunity to help supervise an excavation on the western defences of Roman Lincoln.

Arriving at what then appeared – in comparison with both Manchester and my native South Yorkshire – to be a gentle and rather peaceful sort of town, I had come for a reconnaissance visit to the site at The Park. Previous experience of archaeological sites had not prepared me for the impressive nature of what had already been exposed. Part of the late Roman city wall and adjacent gate-towers were emerging in a remarkable state of preservation, due both to the quality of their build and to their re-use in the city's later fortifications.

For the next two summers, and for some shorter spells in between (when my researches allowed), I spent several months involved in the excavation of the site at The Park, in addition to that further up the hill on West Parade, as well as on a brief emergency job above the hill behind the Eastgate Hotel. All were concerned primarily with Roman defensive features, but there was much else besides, of Roman and later date. All were also deeply stratified sites, the earliest deposits lying several metres below the present ground level. In a short while, I had become entranced with the gratifying richness of Lincoln's archaeology.

The early 1970s were an exhilarating time to be involved in the pioneering, 'heroic' age of rescue archaeology. Activity in the field was expanding rapidly as the destructive impact of development in town and country alike was for the first time matched by a substantial response in terms of public funding. Units of full-time field archaeologists were being established to cope with the demand, and their brief was the complete history of settlement, not merely that of the Roman period. Until 1970, excavations in Lincoln had been the concern of the Museum Curator, but now there was an accepted need for a separate organisation. My research days at Manchester over, I was delighted to join the newly founded Lincoln Archaeological Trust in October 1972 as deputy to Christina Colyer.

Subsequently, having been Director of the Trust and its successor Unit for over 20 years until recently, this year is my thirtieth in the city. I now work as City Archaeologist in the offices of the City Council, overlooking the site which we first excavated in 1970. Lincoln is certainly no longer such a quiet place, with the loss of manufacturing being replaced by a dynamic service sector including higher education. The emphasis of the archaeologist's role is now to preserve rather than investigate, to assess the significance of what survives, and to interpret it for the local community, visitors and educational groups. While some investigations are still occasioned by development proposals, and new discoveries are emerging from the ground, the huge job of preparing the detailed reports on and archives of past excavations is, although well advanced, far from complete. Sufficient data are now available, however, for us to make statements about the past which were not previously possible without the dated sequences and larger sample from the excavations of the past thirty years, including the results of scientific and environmental analysis and a collection of organic material. These provide a more balanced picture.

The development of archaeological theory, much borrowed from the social sciences and of varying levels of applicability, and still an area of lively academic debate, has brought advances in terms of understanding the context of the finds in relation to the everyday lives and thoughts of past communities. At least, we no longer make the same simplistic assumptions about the material. For instance, there is a realization of how much threads of 'ritual' and competitive behaviour ran through various activities, that is, how far people were motivated by irrational beliefs and by their wish to identify themselves as belonging to or leading a particular group. Within the study of Lincoln's long past, in which the significance of the archaeology of the modern industrial era is now fully recognised, the Roman period may now be considered only as a relatively brief episode, even as an interlude. There has been another significant shift in perspective: whereas those generations who were educated primarily in the Classics would have identified with the Roman elite's viewpoint on the conquest and occupation of Britain, the post-Imperial generation to which I just about belong takes a different view of the Roman presence and its benefits. The concept of 'Romanisation' is now seen as outdated, but just how Roman and native populations and influences interacted is still the subject of much research and discussion. Nor was the process unchanging: the Roman period in Britain lasted over 350 years, still excites interest and admiration – notably for its engineering achievements – and has left us remains of a disproportionate amount of the material culture of its elite classes – in other words, it is a period which is highly 'archaeologically visible'. The less visible aspects of life in the Roman settlement are only beginning to emerge.

One challenge of this book, the first full-length treatment of Roman Lincoln, will be to explain how all these remains related the daily life of the Roman community. It has therefore to strike a balance between narrative and analysis. There are those who consider a study of a single city of little value, but this takes no account of our responsibility to explain the story of Lincoln to the local community and its visitors. I have aimed the book primarily at the interested non-specialist, but it may also be found to be of use by students wishing to acquaint themselves with the current state of knowledge. The forthcoming Lincoln Archaeological Research Assessment, being prepared in conjunction with English Heritage, will be altogether a larger and more detailed treatment, and the place to look for further information. Both works owe a great deal to many in the past – whether the early antiquarians, the first systematic excavations carried out from the 1940s by a series of distinguished museum curators and local volunteers, or the thousands who have subsequently taken part in the many excavations carried out since the 1970s and their subsequent analysis. The first chapter tells something of their story.

M.J.J.
Lincoln, August 2002

1 Introduction: Roman Lincoln lost and found

It is now more than 1,500 years since the demise of Roman Lincoln: by AD 450 it had ceased to exist as an urban centre with a sizeable population. Its physical remains, on the other hand, survived well for several centuries, and some elements – notably the city wall – influenced the topography of subsequent periods until the nineteenth century; parts are still visible today.

The earliest antiquaries to remark on Lincoln's visible heritage were, of course, primarily struck by the city's huge Cathedral and other medieval monuments. The existence of these owed much to the fact that Lincoln was a thriving centre at the time of the Norman Conquest, and in turn the earlier decision of the Scandinavian settlers to occupy the site was linked to the existence of a walled enclosure adjacent to a river.

The value of the Roman inheritance was probably appreciated even earlier. In the fourth century, a shift in official priorities led to some monuments being demolished or discarded to make way for enlarged fortifications, whose thickened walls incorporated many re-used architectural fragments and tombstones. The strength of the defences was a factor in the continued or renewed occupation of the site in the next few centuries. Apart from their practical value as a deterrent, the existence of the impressive wall circuit and some substantial (but decaying) buildings within provided a symbolic context for the new Anglo-Saxon warlords and bishops to legitimate their position. Not that Lincoln was necessarily the only, or even principal, base of the Kings of Lindsey: to the Anglo-Saxons, major urban centres were unnecessary, and the king would have owned residences in several places.

The Viking settlement from c.880 involved the replanning and rebuilding (in timber) of parts of the city, initially the south-eastern quadrant of the lower walled city. Excavations have demonstrated that stone and other building materials from ruinous Roman structures proved to be useful for metalling roads and paths, and internal surfaces, while Roman artefacts were used as raw material for metalworking. Surviving walls could serve as lean-tos and prolong existing building-lines and boundaries. The earliest stone structures, the parish churches of the later tenth century, incorporated some re-used fragments, including tombstones, both in foundations and in visible walls: a grave marker found in the Cathedral area was made from a Roman architectural block. More iconic in function were Roman sculptures and tombstones set into prominent positions in church towers of the eleventh century: their presence symbolised the long Roman inheritance and their new location the triumph of Christianity over paganism. In political terms, the occupation of the former Roman upper city as the first Norman castle, and the rebuilding and embellishment of its gates, can be seen as an indication of an awareness of the Roman tradition and the value of imitating it, even six centuries later. Even with the increased use of stone for building, and the development of new quarries and a masonry tradition associated with the Cathedral, the easy availability of Roman walls and foundations meant that they were still being extensively robbed as a source of stone.

The general enlightenment stimulated by the Renaissance led in due course to an interest in physical remains, and tours by travelling scholars who described historic remains. The earliest traveller to Lincoln, the Tudor antiquary John Leland, came in 1544. He noted several features including gates (most of them medieval), bridges, and churches, and finds of Roman coins. William Camden's *Britannia*, first published in 1586, succeeded in achieving the national coverage which illness had prevented Leland from completing. It was revised and enlarged by later scholars: first by Edmund Gibson in 1695, and again in 1722 when he was Bishop of Lincoln. The next edition by Richard Gough of 1789 (reprinted in 1806), is much fuller, covering not only the city walls and gates, but other structures visible and recently uncovered, including the line and possible source of the aqueduct, a house with a hypocaust (under-floor heating system) found adjacent to Exchequergate (**1**), and part of a baths-suite in the yard of the former King's Arms near to the top of High Street.

Some of Gough's descriptions relied heavily on the work of others, notably two eighteenth-century antiquarians: William Stukeley, a physician from south Lincolnshire, and Thomas Sympson, Clerk of Works, Librarian, and Proctor of Lincoln Cathedral. Stukeley too covered much of the country, recording traces of archaeological sites visible in the landscape. At Lincoln he identified and described some of the surviving Roman remains, and wrote in 1724: 'I never saw such a fund of antique speculations in any town in England. I heard continually of coyns and urns. . . .' His remarks were partly a consequence of the discovery of former Roman cemeteries as the town was being rebuilt and expanded, served by new stone quarries being opened at the edge of the existing city. Some of the quarry pits are visible on the map which Stukeley produced (probably based on a visit in 1722) together with his friend Joseph Banks II (grandfather of Sir Joseph, the famous botanist, mentioned below). For several centuries the city had undergone a long period of economic gloom, and various visitors, among them Daniel Defoe, reported on its sorry physical state. But things were on the upturn, especially in the area above the hill in and around the upper Roman city. Artists visited the city in the eighteenth century partly to depict its historic buildings – notably the Cathedral itself – and remains: they form a valuable, and in some cases unique, record of certain monuments. However, not all can be taken at face value: Nathan Drake's view of the (upper) South Gate on Steep Hill, made about 1740, was not one which could actually be seen, since the blocked arch shown had stood inside a building erected in the sixteenth century. Landscape artists did take such liberties, and Drake may have been elaborating on what was

1 *Remains of Roman hypocaust found to south of Exchequergate (west of cathedral), at the then Precentory, in 1740.* Lincolnshire Archives Office

visible inside the building and what he had been told by Thomas Sympson. Sympson later published his records, and they form a valuable source, together with his private collection of artefacts and artworks.

These eighteenth-century accounts are essential to our understanding. The rebuilding of the city was now moving forward and survivals from earlier periods were increasingly at risk. To take one example, the Roman city wall on the west side of Broadgate was still standing. Sympson noted that it was 'miserably peeled and excoriated', while Stukeley's *Itinerarium Curiosum* (revised, 1776 edition) notes a long stretch up to 18 feet high. Within a century all this section had been cleared at least to ground level. His map also indicates the other areas where the wall had survived.

The Georgian period in Lincoln did not witness a comprehensive rebuilding of the city, but saw much physical change. Following the re-opening of the Foss Dyke canal in 1744, by the later decades of the eighteenth century large new edifices were rising, among them a new prison inside the Castle. Lindum Road (the 'New Road') had replaced the medieval Pottergate in 1786, and in the following year finds had been made from the River Witham east of the city. Many artefacts ended up in private hands. Sir Joseph Banks (now a distinguished fellow of the Royal Society) was interested in collecting antiquities as a form of 'relaxation', and professed himself keen to ensure that they were preserved and ordered in the same way as botanical samples, although this was not really possible before they were satisfactorily classified. He managed, by advertising in the local press, to obtain the artefacts from the river, but then, in the spirit of scientific enquiry, he allowed some to be destroyed by chemical analysis. More stunning finds were made when dredging operations took place in 1826 to widen and deepen the Witham to accommodate an increasing amount of traffic. Some were lost; fortunately, many have ended up either in the collections of the City and County Museum, founded in 1906, or that of the British Museum. One other family of eighteenth-century antiquarians deserves mention here: the Pownalls, who lived in Pottergate, east of the Cathedral. William Pownall noted finds of Roman burials as quarrying extended eastwards in the direction of Greetwell. His two sons, John and Thomas ('Governor') Pownall, continued these interests.

The pace of discovery increased and was maintained throughout the nineteenth century as Lincoln's expansion accelerated and much rebuilding took place (some in classical style). New foundations and basements were built, and buried remains were found and removed. There was, moreover, a wider interest in the finds, many of which were noted in the local newspaper, the *Lincoln, Rutland and Stamford Mercury*. Among the more memorable discoveries uphill was the West Gate, revealed ironically when the landlord of the adjacent inn was extending his garden in 1836: it was depicted by two different artists before it began to collapse and was re-covered, as it has remained, except for minor investigations in 1955 (see cover).

Construction work on the line of the City Wall came across many of the sculpted and inscribed stones, some of them tombstones, which had been incorporated into its fourth-century rebuilding. Legionary tombstones also turned up off lower High Street, particularly in the area around Monson Street, an indicator of a legionary cemetery. The building of a reservoir north of Westgate also yielded artefacts associated with the legionary occupation, but since techniques at the time were not adequate to identify the decayed traces of timber buildings the significance of their location was not appreciated for another century. In the Bailgate area the existence of a sewer system was revealed in a cellar in 1838; forty years later, the construction of new cellars and sewers revealed the Bailgate colonnade, now considered to be the frontage of the forum, the civic centre (**35**). More building remains, mosaics and hypocausts turned up, not only on the hilltop, but also on the hillside and even outside the walls (**colour plate 1**). Some of these were explained to the Annual Meeting held in Lincoln in 1848 of the Royal Archaeological Institute, founded only a few years previously, which was a major social event lasting a whole week. An exhibition of 'antiquities' was also held at the meeting's base at the County Assembly Rooms, and the members were shown the specially cleared Roman 'tunnel' (i.e. the sewer) beneath the then Antelope Inn on Bailgate.

An enlightened engineer, Michael Drury, recorded excavations in 1877-8 for the new sewers along the full length of High Street, noting the depth of the causeway of the Roman road – observations which have been useful in recent reconstructions of the early river-courses (**2**). He also saw traces of the early bridge or causeway across the river, a possible dock, and many other buried structures within the walled area. The quality of his recording, including colour representations of buried strata, was exemplary for the period. Edward (E.J.) Willson, a local architect who became Mayor, also left many detailed records and accurate drawings: these have survived well as a

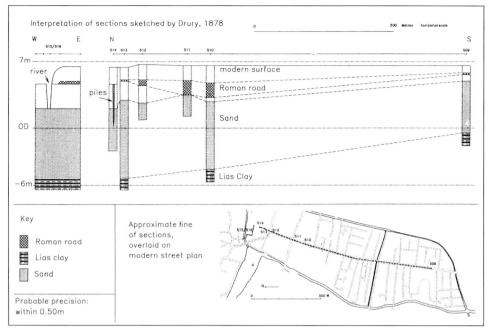

2 *Interpretation of Michael Drury's drawings, showing relative depths of clay and sand deposits, and depth of material dumped to create a level Roman road over damp ground*

source which is much used in the study of the medieval city, but many Roman remains and discoveries are included. The most spectacular Roman residence to be uncovered was the so-called Greetwell Villa, revealed during ironstone quarrying a mile east of the walled city. It was carefully recorded, again to a high standard for the time, by Mr B. Ramsden, quarry manager (**colour plate 14**). The significance of its great scale and the quality of its mosaic pavements is only now being appreciated.

An inevitable consequence was a huge collection of material. Some still went out of Lincoln: the artefacts owned by E.J. Willson were purchased by the Duke of Northumberland, while those collected by the brothers Edward and Arthur Trollope were taken by the British Museum. Finally, in 1906 the creation of the City and County Museum in the Greyfriars building provided a local home.

By the twentieth century, it was possible to produce coherent essays on the Roman occupation of Lincoln. One of the first (though sadly never published) was drafted by the distinguished ancient historian Francis Haverfield, whose writings on Roman Britain are still valued. Meanwhile, discoveries continued: legionary finds from the Water Tower built in 1910 following a typhoid epidemic, early burials on South Common, remains of more private houses and public baths. F.T. ('Tom') Baker was inspired at the age of 14 by the finding of a baths-suite during the construction of Boots' new premises on High Street in 1925, and his appointment as an Assistant in the Museum proved a significant step forward (**3**). He was on hand to record chance discoveries, including the pottery kiln producing *mortaria* (mixing bowls) on the site of the Technical College on Monks Road in 1936. Shortly afterwards, Tom

3 *Hypocaust of the Roman baths at the junction of Clasketgate and High Street, 1925*

Baker produced a booklet on *Roman Lincoln* (1938) for the Historical Association, including the first systematic map of the city which indicated where finds of structures and burials had been made. His suggested grid pattern for the upper city was partly inspired by that of the almost contemporary colony at Timgad in Algeria; he was not to know until a decade later that the legionary fortress lay immediately beneath the upper city.

The remains of the fortress began to emerge in excavations carried out under the supervision of Graham Webster, then an engineer based in Lincoln but in due course to become a Roman archaeologist of great repute. The momentum had continued during the Second World War, with investigations of several kiln sites on the edge of town. The meeting of the Royal Archaeological Institute in Lincoln in 1946, almost a century after the first, proved another watershed. With support from Haverfield's notes and Tom Baker's researches, Ian Richmond, soon to become the leading figure in Roman archaeology in Britain, wrote a detailed essay for publication in the Institute's journal, together with a discussion of the other *coloniae*. Although understandably now out of date in many ways, it remains a fundamental contribution. At the same time, the establishment of the Lincoln Archaeological Research Committee (LARC), with a programme of objectives set out by Richmond in 1945, created a framework for another twenty years of targeted endeavour. These objectives included the definition of the site of the legionary fortress, its defences, and its internal structures; for the *colonia* he set as priorities the elucidation of the structure(s) represented by the Mint Wall and the Bailgate colonnade; the plans of the gates, the street-plan and its relationship to the sewer system; the water supply; dating for the colony's foundation; the nature and date of its growth outside the original enclosure, and the types of structures found in the lower enclosure. Richmond was impressed by the apparently cosmopolitan nature of the population and metropolitan influences discernible in the sculptures, art, and other material, which encouraged him to write: 'Roman Lincoln itself offers a glimpse of flourishing Roman urban culture in imported purity such as has not yet emerged anywhere else on British provincial soil.' Like many of Richmond's elegant statements, it acted as a stimulus to those in Lincoln and elsewhere. In the light of more recent discoveries in other cities, it is a judgement which can no longer be sustained, for several other Romano-British sites can claim evidence for similar artistic quality, and the imported culture was largely that of the north-west provinces rather than the Mediterranean.

The sites available to the LARC in 1945 were numerous, not because of bombing during the war which had only touched Lincoln lightly, but following a sustained programme of slum clearance. In Graham Webster's report on the first two seasons' work he described discoveries of no fewer than eight different sites, plus others outside the city boundary. Many excavations were problematic because of the great depth of stratigraphy (and post-Roman deposits were sometimes poorly recorded), but happily at Westgate the legionary defences survived close to the ground (**4**).

Following Graham Webster's departure to the Curatorship of Chester Museum, Tom Baker oversaw the contributions made by a series of museum curators over the following three decades – in turn Hugh Thompson, Dennis Petch, and Ben Whitwell – who as far as possible followed the guidelines set by Richmond. The outline of the fortress was confirmed by excavations on all sides, while inside the city a public fountain, public baths and other structures were revealed (**5**). Beyond the

4 *The Roman legionary ditch, and to its left (east), the front palisade trench for the rampart as found in 1945-6 by Graham Webster.* Photograph by I.A. Richmond

walls, more kilns were investigated and the aqueduct at least partially understood. Increasingly, however, as the pace of development in the city quickened, prior attention had to be given to sites where new construction offered unrepeatable opportunities for recording.

This work was still undertaken with the help of volunteers, often working only evenings and weekends, and a few workmen. By 1970, the scale of change was such that other arrangements had to be made, and the job of excavation was professionalised and separated from the duties of the museum. In 1972, in line with developments in other towns, a full-time team was established: the Lincoln Archaeological Trust. Its initial Chairman and Secretary, Sir Francis Hill and Tom Baker, were the same two important figures who had set up the LARC 37 years previously. Its first Director, Christina Colyer, who had already overseen excavations in the city from 1970, and her staff, were invariably young and idealistic – just as in the many similar organisations which were being formed elsewhere, as the fledgling world of rescue archaeology expanded exponentially, partly fuelled by central government funding. Given their daunting work programme, great energy was essential, and over the next two decades more sites were excavated and more finds made than during the previous two centuries. The approach, inspired by the Winchester Research Unit, was more comprehensive than the largely Roman-period concerns of the LARC: to study the origins of the city and its development from the earliest settlement to its characteristic modern form. With improved recording techniques and increasing scientific support, new dimensions were added to our understanding, more valid samples were obtained, and problematic remains could be interpreted. It was this period that saw a late Iron Age settlement discovered, and a realisation that the Roman street system had largely been lost before replanning in the late Saxon and Norman periods. The recovery of detailed sequences and sufficient remains of building plans at least to characterise areas of the city – including extensive suburbs – and in certain cases to plot individual structures, represented major steps forward. A slightly later development stemmed partly from investigating riverfronts: waterlogged deposits yielded large groups of organic materials, both artefacts of wood and leather, and biological samples which highlighted the hitherto-neglected environmental aspects. It allowed us to begin to produce a more balanced picture of the realities of an urban centre.

The analysis of the vast amount of data and material which emerged, and which is still emerging from the ground, has not kept pace with their discovery, and while there have been a number of thematic publications and detailed reports, the publication of this material is still on-going. Its collection in a database, which will be made generally accessible, will allow others to study the evidence, and perhaps to draw different conclusions. This delay has had some positive effects, for instance, in allowing account to be taken of new advances in archaeological thinking. The problem of dating features when so many of the associated finds are residual, in other words, when they are derived from earlier deposits, has been addressed. In theoretical terms, the recognition of how images and buildings could be used to particular effect is influencing modern interpretations.

5 *The Newport Arch almost destroyed by a lorry in 1964. Looking north.*
Copyright *Lincolnshire Echo*

In the study of Roman Britain, the contribution of the native aristocracy had been underestimated; there is now a greater understanding of the influence of the native population as a whole, and a closer relationship is acknowledged between the locations of Roman military bases and the concentrations of native settlement. It is true that, in higher educational circles in Britain, the Roman period no longer holds such dominance over earlier or later periods as it did only a generation ago – and perhaps deservedly so. But the fact that the Roman presence lasted almost 400 years, during which time nothing stayed the same, means that there is much more to be understood of the processes at work, and the transitional phases at the beginning and end of the period are still lively areas of research. Any political and economic system is inherently unstable, and radical changes might be brought about by environmental factors such as climate and landscape change as much as political or economic ones.

As noted above, sub-Roman warlords found a Roman identity of political value. Even now, a study of Roman Lincoln represents a combination of local, national and international history. It will, I hope, be appreciated by modern readers at all three levels. The distinguished ancient historian, Sir Moses Finley, wrote in 1985 that we did not need more single-town monographs, especially if they were descriptive in their approach, but rather studies which illuminated the workings of the Roman imperial system or at least present new approaches to the understanding of the past. But since our evidence is so fragmentary, each city has its own particular contribution to make to the whole – 'all history is local history'. Furthermore, the value of our local heritage is increasingly appreciated for the contribution it makes to life in various ways, and those who inhabit and visit cities like Lincoln deserve to have its own story set out. This book covers just part of that long story.

2 Prologue: before history

Setting: 'the place by the pool'

For all the long list of distinguished commentators on, and investigators of, its remarkable historic remains, described in the previous chapter, and its popularity as a tourist destination, the city of Lincoln is still poorly known. For many, it apparently lies too far east of the main routes to notice, let alone visit. There is a similarly misleading perception that the whole of Lincolnshire (and not just the fens which it shares with adjoining counties to the south) is an unrelieved flat landscape. Many receive a shock on discovering that the city centre at Lincoln contains a daunting hill, at the top of which are the principal historic survivals, sufficiently elevated to make an impression for miles around. The cathedral and its surrounds represent the current popular image of the ancient city, but the earliest settlement actually lay in the valley at the foot of the hill. Its name is derived from that of the Roman city, *Lindum Colonia*, in turn based on the stem 'lindo-', actually a pre-Roman, British word relating to a 'lake' or 'pool'. The Brayford Pool – whose existence is another surprise to first-time visitors – is still a significant feature of the townscape, although the area of open water is much reduced in extent from that existing at the time of the Roman occupation.

The Pool is a basin still considered to have originated as a result of natural processes. It occurs at the point where the rivers Till (later superseded by the Fossdyke canal) and Witham meet, before flowing through a gap in the Jurassic Ridge which has been deepened and widened by glacial action. The Ridge, of oolitic limestone, is here *c*.8km wide, with a steep scarp, the 'Lincoln Edge', on its west side (**6**). Since land forms, and the availability of mineral resources, to some extent shaped the development of the Roman settlement, the creation and development of the natural topography are worth summarising. The Lincoln Gap is still a problem area even for geological experts. It already existed in the Pliocene period (*c*.2 million years ago), when a 'Lincoln River', draining the hills of what is now north Nottinghamshire, flowed eastwards through it and to the coast immediately south of the Wolds – a line much further north than the later seaward course of the Witham. At some stage its tributaries were captured by the Trent. During the succeeding long Pleistocene period, the valley at the Lincoln Gap was deepened on two occasions. The first took place over 100,000 years ago, when an earlier course of the River Trent was diverted by the presence of ice-sheets. Subsequently, the Trent found a lower outlet towards the Humber (a lake also formed by the melting ice), taking with it the Witham tributaries. During a blockage of this course in the Devensian Glaciation (over 50,000 years ago), it temporarily returned to the Witham Gap and again deepened the valley. When the Humber became free of

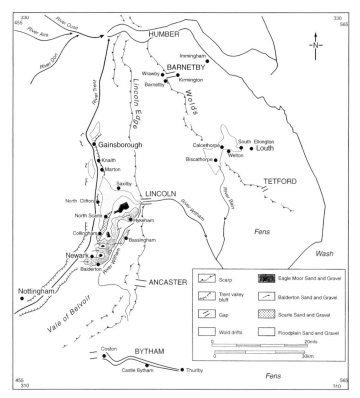

6 *Location of Lincoln in relation to gaps in the Lincoln Edge, and gravel deposition in the Witham and Trent valleys. By courtesy of Alan Straw*

ice, the Trent moved to its present route, this time abandoning the Witham streams. These movements of melting ice also created gravel deposits to the west and south-west of the city, characterised by pools and meres adjacent to the river channels.

So much for geological time, but the landscape was changing throughout prehistory. Subsequently, in Lincoln itself, analysis of samples of peat from buried deposits adjacent to Brayford Pool suggested that by *c.*6000 BC, during the Mesolithic period, there was dry land at only 1m above the present sea level. Lincoln's site was at the mercy of natural forces and the levels rose and fell. From *c.*2000 BC, the formation of extensive peat deposits in the Witham Valley to the east may have resulted from a rise in sea level, possibly exacerbated by run-off from large-scale clearances inland. In parts of the Lincolnshire Fens, the maximum river levels were reached about 1400 BC, and may then have remained fairly static for several hundred years. An estuarine creek system identified several miles downstream of the city can probably be dated to this era, with the sea probably penetrating as far as Short Ferry, east of Fiskerton, *c.*10km from Lincoln (**7**). The Brayford Pool was a lake, possibly surrounded by an area of marsh: tidal influence in the city is documented by the existence of 'Fen Clay', noted in excavations on the east side of the Pool, which appears to have been deposited here in the second millennium BC. The sea covered part of the fens, but the exact line of the coast is difficult to establish, since the land was partly marsh and swamp prone to flooding. The coastline to the north of the Fens has, in contrast, been prone to erosion since the Roman period, and some important settlements may have been lost.

Peat growth in the Witham valley continued into the Iron Age, but at some date in the middle of the first millennium BC levels began to fall. By the early Roman period, the Brayford Pool area may have reverted to marsh, subject to seasonal flooding adjacent to the river courses. The Pool was still much more extensive than today, appears to have contained several islands, or areas of higher ground, and may have been linked to other pools nearby. There was a further rise in level during the later Roman period, possibly again linked to that of the sea, but alternatively caused by an artificial barrier. At the edge of the Pool, land has been reclaimed successively over several centuries. The evidence of the species of molluscs and diatoms (unicellular algae) from excavated sites in the city indicates that the river flow was mostly slow or moderate, with only occasional hints of marine influence. The river system, it must be said, is still unstable: only in recent years have flood–alleviation schemes been implemented to offer assurances to those who reside below the 10m contour – and that means many in the lower part of town (the 'Wigford' area, named after the medieval suburb), and other points adjacent to the water up- and down-stream. The latest episodes of flooding, possibly associated with global warming but also caused by intensive agriculture, are necessitating a renewed programme of riverbank strengthening, with concomitant opportunities for archaeological research.

The gap itself at Lincoln is about 2km wide, being narrower *c.*5km to the east, and must have formed a significant local landmark. Poorly draining, steep scarps rise to the limestone ridge either side of the valley at a height of *c.*60m above sea level. Lias clay is accessible on the hillside, a useful source for pottery and bricks. The ridge

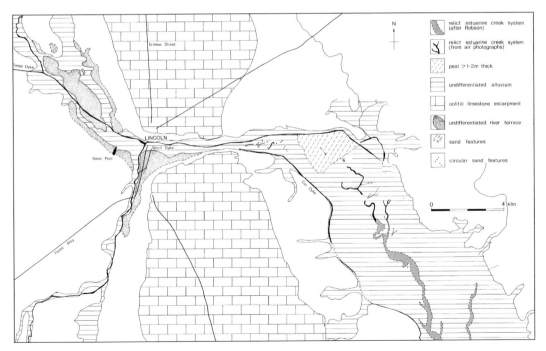

7 *The Lincoln area, showing terrace deposits, the Witham Gap, and the early estuarine creek system to the east, with some Bronze Age round-barrows visible as sand features.* T. Wilkinson

itself is capped with limestone suitable for building and sculpture, and this gave a distinctive physical character to the built environment of the Roman (and medieval) city which is still clearly apparent in the core of the historic town today. On the hilltop, close to its western scarp and overlooking the gap to the south, was the site of the legionary fortress and succeeding upper walled city, with suburbs to north, east and west. The tabular bedrock, some of which was quarried during the Roman period, only occurs (in varying beds of different quality for building) at some depth, normally of a few metres, except on the edge of the cliff. It is usually covered by a 'corn brash' subsoil of small rubble mixed with a light-coloured clay on average about 1m thick, and sometimes mixed with or sealed by an orange-brown, blown sand. This sand can also fill surface geological features, with a resulting confusion for excavators who might otherwise interpret them as structural features: Graham Webster thought that he had encountered 'Iron Age rock-cut postholes' during his excavations on the western defences in the 1940s, but later realised that the features were of geological origin. A 15m-deep investigation of the fuller sequence was achieved during 1984 when the well in the east range of the Roman forum was emptied. This indicated a limestone deposit *c*.8m thick beneath the brash, overlying *c*.3m of Northampton ironstone on top of the Lias clay.

The 'Lower Walled City' occupies the northern scarp of the Gap between the river and the hilltop, sitting on the clay and some limestone and ironstone nearer to the top – the break between them in the form of a limestone cliff apparently being visible in places in the nineteenth century. The clay on the steeper part of the slope, which requires terracing, was formerly characterised by springs, streams and ponds, which drained badly. There is a significant change to sandy terraces lower down: the sandy deposits, in contrast, drain well. The archaeological deposits on the steeper hillside can either be very deeply buried or in places shallow, or even completely removed by later terracing. The deepest deposits occur in the lower half of the hillside, where they average 4-5m, while those in the upper walled city can reach a depth of 3-4m. Nineteenth-century borings are reported to have exposed 'peaty alluvium' near to the Stonebow, just north of the contemporary river line, its surface at *c*.8-9m OD: one may infer from this information, supported by Michael Drury's illustration, that the north bank of the river may originally have lain north of the lower defences. Alternatively, it may represent colluvium: this is not peat, but silty material eroded from higher up the slope. Its identification cannot be confirmed.

The sand is also found at various heights in the southern suburb of Wigford. The position close to the waterside, however, is more complicated, having two river-terraces – former flood-plains – which were noted by early geologists as well as the recent excavations. The first, at *c*.4.8m OD, is by the railway crossing over High Street, which must represent an area of higher land of uncertain extent; and another at *c*.3.2-3.5m OD, which was later sealed by the dumps of earth deposited in the late second century AD to make the ground suitable for settlement. Michael Drury noted that a causeway up to *c*.1.5m thick had needed to be constructed in order to carry the Roman road over the lower terrace (**2**). Other early geological investigations noted that higher terracing occurred further south again, at 5.5m OD, characterised by 'white or estuarine sand', and a further 'island' to the south-west. The terraces indicate the lowering of the river bed by glacial action. As a result of these observations, and those made during the recent Waterside excavations, we can define the approximate edge of the river and Pool in the mid- to late Roman period.

In summary, all three separate elements of the ancient city had disadvantages from the point of view of settlement – whether liable to flooding, difficult to drain, or difficult to supply. On the other hand, the location had strategic benefits from the point of view of the Roman army, in addition to those available to any pre-existing community: the wetland was a rich source of food and useful for transport.

Prehistoric settlement

Lincoln has traditionally been perceived as a settlement created entirely by the Romans, based on its strategic advantages for military control. This view was valid until relatively recently: the city had produced no evidence for pre-Roman settlement until in 1972 investigation south of the river uncovered traces of Late Iron Age occupation. Although the native dimension had been largely ignored, some authorities had always suggested that the Roman army took note of concentrations of existing settlements when choosing the locations of their bases. There is now an increasing awareness of the Iron Age background of much of Romano-British settlement.

The remains of the earliest settlement of the Lincoln area are slight, vulnerable, deeply buried, and, not surprisingly, are only emerging slowly. We still have too little evidence to understand how early occupation began, how extensive it was, and what was its exact character. Chance finds of early prehistoric stone implements from the city do not provide definite clues. The pattern of their distribution showed no great clusters in Lincoln, but interestingly most came from the east side of the city in or close to the valley, perhaps hinting at the significance of the narrower part of the Gap. Lincoln lies on the line of the long-distance route known as the Jurassic Way, which may have been used from the time of the earliest settlers in the Mesolithic or Neolithic period. Where it crossed the gap is open to question, but the origin of the city's name is further confirmation that the water was a main focus of early activity. The location of the city at the head of the fens also meant that the extent of the water varied, as it was subject at times to influence from changing sea levels.

The River Till appears to have flowed to the south of the line of its successor, the Fossdyke canal, and along the southern side of the Brayford Pool before joining the course of the Witham. Sampling of the buried peats on the south side of the existing Pool, undertaken in 1994 in connection with the development of the University campus, produced some useful information on the early landscape. The peat samples were particularly rich in plant and invertebrate remains, indicating a natural wetland with developing reed swamp, fen carr and raised bog. Two samples, both containing much oak and alder pollen, were dated approximately by radiocarbon to the Neolithic and Bronze Ages: 2850 BC and 1150 BC (dates subject to calibration). Plotting of the occurrence of the peat and other deposits has enabled James Rackham to identify not only the early line of the River Till, but also a higher area of sand, at times almost an island in what was then a larger pool. A subsequent series of samples taken from various sites around the Brayford indicates that peat formation began as early as the Mesolithic period, before 6000 BC, at a time when even the sandy areas as low as *c*.1m OD may have been habitable. There was almost no indication from the early peat deposits for human activity, but that does not necessarily mean that the Pool was not significant in the life of any local inhabitants.

The sampling programme is ongoing, as sites around the Brayford Pool undergo redevelopment, and it may in due course prove possible to investigate what remains of the sand 'island' to the south-west of the present Pool for any traces of early settlement. There were probably other areas of high land further to the south-west which would repay investigation, but the prehistoric settlement of the Lincoln area cannot be understood in an isolated context. In providing a conceptual framework for the evidence to date from the city, as part of preparing the Lincoln Archaeological Research Assessment, David Stocker has drawn attention to the significance of the finds east of the city, and to their ritual nature. During the earlier part of the Bronze Age (second millennium BC), many burial-mounds, in the form of round barrows, were built on both sides of the river. Their existence was being noted by the eighteenth century, when several cremation urns were found. A large group of barrows lying a mile or so to the east of the city centre is visible on aerial photographs. These features occur mainly outside the present city boundary, in the parishes of Greetwell and Canwick, but probably extended closer to Lincoln: they may be obscured, or have been obliterated, by industrial development. Another concentration of round barrows is apparent 3km downstream, beyond Washingborough village. Evidence for Early Bronze Age occupation on the higher ground is less substantial, but a few finds of urns and contemporary artefacts have been made on the hill slopes overlooking the valley.

By the Later Bronze Age, there had been a rise in sea level, perhaps compounded by clearances upstream, and extensive peat deposits formed along the Witham Valley, affecting the barrow sites. From this period, prestigious metal objects were deposited in the river or in pools adjacent to it. This is a phenomenon not peculiar to the Witham Valley: there are many similar finds from the River Thames, for instance, and at the remarkable site at Flag Fen, on the eastern edge of Peterborough. The practice continued for many centuries, into the Iron Age and beyond. The occurrence of these metal objects was possibly linked in some way with the occurrence of boat finds from the same stretch of the river (**8**), and may have been associated with burial in water, or at least sacrifice. It is now generally accepted that the finds were not casual losses but deliberate offerings, made to enhance the donor's standing in society or possibly to commemorate an important event in the life of that society. The places from which deposition was undertaken may have been artificial causeways, such as that of fifth- to fourth-century BC date found at Fiskerton, *c*.8km east of Lincoln, in 1981. Two Iron Age dug-out canoes and other objects were found associated with the causeway in 2001.

Some exotic finds have been made in the river east of the city, but the precise locations are uncertain. The causeway at Stamp End is known to have existed in the medieval period, but David Stocker and Paul Everson have discerned a whole series

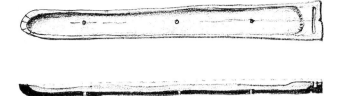

8 *Log-boat from Short Ferry*

originating in the late Bronze Age downstream of Lincoln, and suggested that the 20 prehistoric metal objects recovered from the river during work on the bank and channel in 1787-8 and 1826 may have come from the river adjacent to this causeway. Those artefacts included five swords, mostly of late Bronze Age date, but there were notable later finds, of which the Witham Shield was the finest. The quality of workmanship on the Shield, probably made in the third to second centuries BC, makes it one of the outstanding pieces of Iron Age art in Britain (**colour plate 4**).

The votive deposits of the Witham Valley add a potentially religious dimension to the late Iron Age structures and artefacts found in 1972 at 181-3 High Street, *c.*200m south of the present river line, and over 100m east of the present Brayford Pool. At the time these were unexpected discoveries, and initially assumed to represent domestic occupation. The remains were found on a sandy knoll of higher ground at an elevation of *c.*4.8m OD. The nature of their location on an 'island' was only recognised subsequently. The excavations revealed various structural features, including an eavesdrip gully defining a circular house (**9**), and two sides of a rectangular timber structure represented by post-holes, probably from the period between *c.*100 BC and the Roman Conquest. The structural remains resemble those found at other late Iron Age sites in the county: Dragonby, Colsterworth and Ancaster. Among the native style pottery from 181-3 High Street were vessels dated to the first century BC – notably a burnished and decorated globular jar, of a type found also at Dragonby. Other objects, including a brooch, may also have been of pre-Roman origin. Animal bones from the early deposits reinforce the view that natives used the site in the earliest phases, based on the range of species represented and evidence of butchery techniques. Since so little of the site was accessible for investigation, the ritual use of the water downstream suggests the alternative possibility that here too was a sacred site rather than domestic occupation, but none of the objects found can

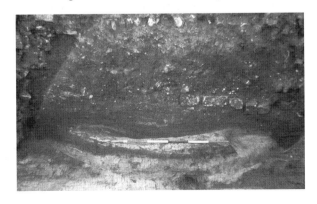

9 *Excavations at 181-3 High Street, 1972. Eaves-drip gully of part of a circular house, built on the sand island*

definitely be interpreted as a votive offering, and more investigations are required before this matter can be settled (**colour plate 6**).

As yet, the evidence does not add up to a major concentration of settlement (**10**). On the analogy of the *oppida*, the Late Iron Age tribal centres of south-east England, such settlements could spread over a large area – not that this meant that the land was not valued or uncontrolled. They might consist of areas for settlement and agriculture, an enclosure on high ground, and separate foci for ritual activities including burial: rituals were often associated with water. One definite element of note at Lincoln was the extensive linear ditch system traced at several locations to the north and north-east of the city. Double or triple ditches and their associated banks, with occasional gaps, extended from the Greetwell area north-westwards to the west of Nettleham. The best-preserved examples of these ditches were in places more than 1.5m deep, and associated with counterscarp banks: the earthen banks would in fact have represented the more visible aspect in the landscape. They may have divided up the land. Several interpretations for their construction are possible, including a symbolic one – such features as trackways, for controlling people, stock movement, and access to water. The gaps in the ditches, at which other features including structures were found, may have been connected with these operations, which may have had a ritual element. One recent investigation suggested that not all the ditches were in use at the same time, and that one of them was filled before the second century BC. A date possibly as early as the late Bronze Age, and certainly no later than early to middle Iron Age date, seems likely for the construction of the system: in that case

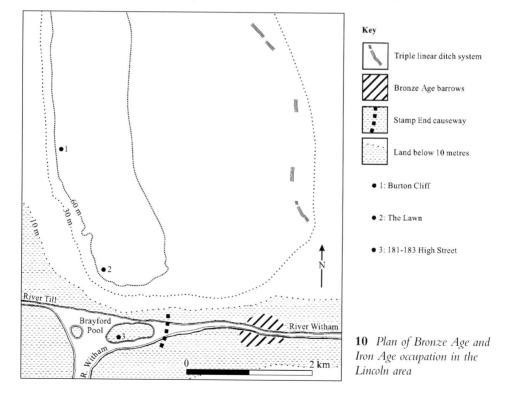

10 *Plan of Bronze Age and Iron Age occupation in the Lincoln area*

there may have been some relationship to the events on the river, marked by the causeways and the votive offerings. Final backfilling, or natural infilling, appears to have occurred early in the Roman period.

No other definite Iron Age structures have been found in the city itself: this is perhaps not surprising, given the slight nature of the evidence and the long history of subsequent occupation. It is difficult to assess the significance of the collection of native-type pottery of the Conquest period from the grounds of the Lawn (to the west of the uphill fortress – see chapter 5). It included both beakers and bowls. It would be unwise to claim this as being definitely pre-Roman, since its use may have been associated with the presence of the army. It is a further mile to the north-west, towards Burton, before more definite evidence can be reported: pottery of the early first century AD was found in pits revealed during the construction of the Lincoln Relief Road in 1984, suggesting a hilltop settlement in this area. There were certainly other settlements around, both on the heath and on the fen-edge, which continued to be occupied into the Roman period.

Jeffrey May has noted the absence of stratified Iron Age coins from the city, in contrast to several other local settlements such as Owmby (16km north of Lincoln). As yet, the finds from 181-3 High Street and others from the city do not add up to unequivocal evidence for an occupation site. Whether the various remains constitute an *oppidum*, a quasi-urban settlement, is uncertain. May considered that we should be thinking rather in terms of a series of small clusters of settlement similar to the pattern found in some other river valleys, and these might include at least one focus for festivals and ceremonies. The existence of a place-name may indicate a well-known location, and that the name stemmed from the presence of water is a key to the principal focus of interest.

Of course, occupation of whatever type at Lincoln must be seen within the context of the political geography of the tribal region, in the lands of the Corieltauvi, which covered much of the modern East Midlands. The major settlements of the eastern tribal area, i.e. those occupying Lincolnshire and at least north-east Leicestershire, were not defended but open sites, and most show evidence both of growth and of some material wealth in the first century BC – perhaps stimulated by early contacts, facilitated by its coinage, with Gaul and south-east Britain (**11**). This may indicate a stable economic and social system. In analyses based on a study of the abundant finds of coins and on pottery types, Jeffrey May has further developed his ideas on the Late Iron Age in this region. The area between the Humber and the Witham appears to have been the primary area of development, perhaps based mainly on stock raising on the chalk and limestone hills. The availability of iron ore and salt no doubt provided further sources of wealth. The occurrence of stamped and decorated pottery was confined to this northern area until *c.*100 BC, when, perhaps in search of better sea passages, the area south of the Witham was also taken under control from the north and subjected to the same cultural and technological refinements. Lincoln sits on the border of the two regions, and possibly between two groups (or 'septs') of the tribe, and the important route linking them must have crossed the river nearby. The crossing-point may have constituted an important meeting place.

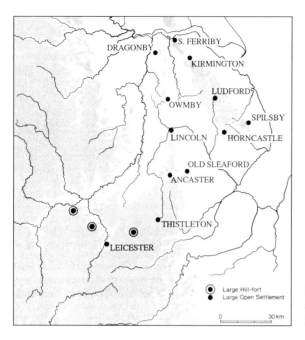

11 *Approximate extent of the territory of the Corieltauvi, indicating some of the settlement sites.* M. Todd

Lincolnshire's Iron Age is at last beginning to receive attention. Apart from the recent Fenland Project and a formal mapping of sites by aerial photography, a major initiative on the Witham Valley is now under way, stimulated by essential strengthening of the flood banks. The new project should help to provide a clearer context for finds from the area of the city. Much new information has also been obtained in recent decades from the investigation and analysis of a number of extensive settlements, those at Dragonby (north of Scunthorpe) and at Old Sleaford being most notable. The second was not only very large but also a major centre of coin production, and, on the evidence of over 4,000 coin moulds, a principal political centre of the Corieltauvi. The tribe had a coinage from *c.*70 BC, which allowed transactions to take place with the elite of other tribes also possessing a currency, and even possibly with the Roman world via Northern Gaul, but it lay on the periphery of those areas with most contact with and influence from Roman culture. The large settlement at Owmby has yielded a good number of Iron Age coins and is characterised by an orderly series of enclosures. It was subsequently the next major Roman settlement site going north from Lincoln along Ermine Street; that a similar distance to the south was Navenby, which, like the next site to the south, Ancaster, has also produced some evidence for settlement in the Late Iron Age. It almost appears as if there was an Iron Age predecessor of Ermine Street. All may also have seen early Roman military occupation (chapter 3), a fact which encourages us to consider to what extent the army's strategy was influenced by the presence of native populations as well as by military considerations.

3 Conquest: the Roman army
in the Lincoln area

The conquest of Britain

The Roman invasion of Britain in AD 43 was driven by the political need to provide a military victory for the recently-installed Emperor Claudius. A pretext was provided by an appeal to Rome from the leader of the Atrebates tribe, Verica, who was being ejected by his rivals. His was one of several tribes which had maintained good relations with Rome since Julius Caesar's visits in 55-54 BC. Their leaders benefited from luxuries such as wine made available through Roman trading networks, and their families – in particular sons sent to Rome for education – were further impressed by the Roman way of life. In effect, the tribal aristocracy of South-East Britain was being seduced – willingly, it must be said – by the attractive material benefits that contact with the Empire could bring. This contact had social and cultural consequences, with greater emphasis being placed on material goods and a taste developed for Mediterranean culture and delicacies.

The invasion, nevertheless, demanded a considerable investment of resources, including four legions and a presumably similar number of auxiliary troops, generally estimated at about 40,000 soldiers in all. They needed to be supplied with food, shelter, and equipment as well as pay, and where these were not available locally they were imported to Britain. Once under occupation, the investment was partially repaid in rich minerals, including gold and silver, in slaves, and in other commodities such as wool and food.

It can be assumed that conquest of the whole of Britain was the aim, bearing in mind that this still meant dealing in diplomatic or military activity with the various tribes. The main landings may have taken place near Richborough, in Kent, or near to Chichester in West Sussex: there is currently a lively dispute between the proponents of each. There were battles south of the River Thames, but after its crossing the army assembled to await the arrival of Claudius himself. The Emperor, accompanied by elephants, went to Camulodunum (Colchester), a major *oppidum* (tribal centre), to receive the formal submission of several British leaders. It is quite conceivable that the Corieltauvi tribe of the East Midlands region was among those represented; although on the periphery of the south-east which had had closest contact with Gaul, they did issue their own coinage based on Roman models.

The Twentieth Legion established a fortress at Colchester, where it remained for six years. The other legions advanced, through a landscape already largely cleared and intensively cultivated: the Second *Augusta* towards the south-west, consolidating after a decade or so at Exeter; the Fourteenth north-westwards, coming together at Wroxeter in Shropshire; and the Ninth *Hispana* (so called after a victorious campaign in Spain) directly northwards, skirting the fringes of the tribal area of the Iceni of East Anglia and into the lands of the Corieltauvi, in due course consolidating at Lincoln. In spite of the acquiescence of the tribal kings, the appearance of the Roman army must have made a deep impression on the natives, as well as its economic and environmental consequences. The invaders were here to stay, their role to offer independence to those who welcomed the conquest, or threats of dark consequences to those who resisted, before the authorities could proceed with the assimilation of each tribal area into the provincial administration.

The occupation of the Corieltauvi

Roman military penetration into the tribal region of the Corieltauvi occurred in the first few years or so after the Roman invasion's landing in AD 43. A distinction should be made between the period of campaigning, using camps and temporary bases which might leave little trace, and that of occupation, for which more permanent forts were needed, linked by roads. The details of the early years of the conquest are still a matter of dispute, but there is now some reason to believe that at least part of the Fourteenth Legion had reached as far as Alchester, Oxfordshire within a year. With regard to Lincoln, however, the date at which it was first selected and occupied as a military base, and whether that first base was the main hilltop fortress, are as yet unresolved questions.

The attitude to the invading army of the local tribe remains uncertain. Its lands were situated between the ostensibly friendly client kingdoms of the Brigantes (a loose federation covering most of what is now northern England) and the Iceni of East Anglia. With a change in ruler, that friendliness was not guaranteed: both of these tribes later rebelled, for their own different reasons, and military action was necessary, with implications for occupation of the Corieltauvi's lands. Certainly there were marching camps and several large forts away from the later military road system: the army may have made use of existing trackways in such circumstances, or have secured supply lines with quickly built routeways. These activities were not necessarily linked to campaigns in the tribal area of the Corieltauvi, which may have agreed to accept Roman authority after a comparatively brief period of negotiation. The large forts of 8-12 hectares – so-called 'vexillation fortresses' – displayed sufficient similarity in planning to suggest that they belong to a particular group, and are usually interpreted as housing legionary detachments (*vexillationes*), perhaps brigaded together with auxiliaries. The various bases of this type so far identified were at Longthorpe west of Peterborough, Osmanthorpe near Newark, Newton-on-Trent west of Lincoln, Rossington Bridge south-east of Doncaster, and possibly at Broxtowe, Nottingham (**12**). Longthorpe, the only site to be investigated on any scale, appears to have been founded soon after the move northwards. It could be interpreted as a base from which the occupation of the Coreltauvi was launched. There are clear ceramic links between Lincoln and Longthorpe, suggesting that potters making red-slipped wares occupied both sites, and perhaps moved with the army from Longthorpe to Lincoln. This link makes it more likely that Longthorpe was indeed a base for part of the Ninth Legion. Detachments may have been housed in winter quarters of this type, perhaps together with auxiliaries in the campaigning seasons. The exact function of these large forts is not fully understood, but there are too many similar sites for them all to have been occupied contemporaneously, and dating evidence from others suggests use into the Neronian period (AD 54-68).

It is possible that the construction of the other sites was part of a strategy to establish a position on the edge of Corieltauvian territory, monitoring any problems issuing from the Brigantes tribe, where there had been internal political problems with possible consequences for the conquest. In this context, the settlement of the full legion at Lincoln would have consolidated the occupation of Corieltauvian territory: Lincoln's site served to block access from the north, with the legion held in reserve behind the contemporary frontier at the Humber and able to keep an eye on both the Brigantes and the Iceni. It was also possible to block the other route from the north, via the lowest crossing of the Trent at Littleborough/Marton, *c*.20km north-west of Lincoln, where a small fort was built; land to the north of that crossing included much wetland.

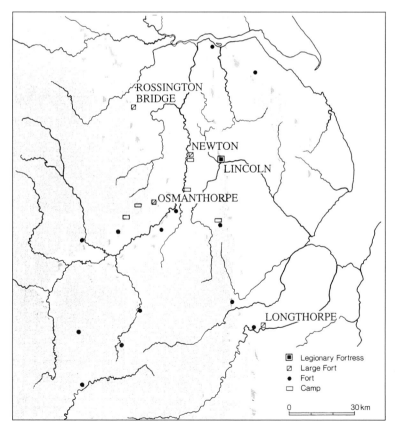

12 *Early military sites in the East Midlands.* M. Todd

The fact that there was an early military route along the Fosse Way linking Lincoln to Exeter has suggested to some that a frontier was established here. Others argue that the line was no more than a strategic communication route which was a secondary development to the main thrusts to the north and west. Landscape analysis by Brian Roberts and Stuart Wrathmell has now added a further dimension, pointing out that this line may have followed the approximate edge of contemporary early forest, which would of course require a different military approach. The Fosse Way and Ermine Street, which joined south of the marshy land and the river crossing at Lincoln, were protected by a series of forts at regular intervals, with extra bases at strategic points. Those identified to date on Ermine Street, which was probably the earlier route, include Great Casterton and Ancaster; and others are perhaps likely at Navenby south of Lincoln, and possibly at Owmby to the north; as was noted in the previous chapter, most were existing centres of native population (**11**, **12**; for site names, see **60**). On the Fosse Way to the south-west of Lincoln there were small forts at Margidunum, Thorpe-by-Newark (*Ad Pontem*), and Brough, but again their foundation dates are uncertain. Other early forts are known, such as that at another native concentration, at Kirmington at a gap in the Wolds. Few have been investigated in sufficient detail to reveal their detailed layout, whilst the military position was fluid; therefore existing methods of dating are of only limited help in assigning them to particular campaigns. As a consequence, interpretations of the Roman strategy and of the chronology of the different campaign phases can differ, and again the distinction between campaigning and occupation needs to be emphasised.

Few of the above sites have provided evidence to indicate that they were occupied before the end of the Claudian period (AD 54), although there is a problem with dating evidence in those years: the regular bronze coinage was not being supplied to Britain. The Ninth Legion may have been subdivided and based initially in marching camps and then in two or more smaller fortresses for several years, and the various detachments only brought together when the hilltop fortress was constructed at Lincoln. The pottery dating from excavations both inside the uphill fortress, and at the earliest sites of extra-mural occupation so far investigated, would favour a foundation date not before the early Neronian period, *c*.AD 55-60, and possibly in *c*.AD 61 following the suppression of the Boudiccan revolt. Other authorities differ: Webster suggested a later Neronian foundation related to a military reorganisation in *c*.AD 66, following the withdrawal from Britain of the Fourteenth Legion. On the basis of the dating of samian pottery, Brian Hartley has proposed an even later date, in the early 70s.

On the evidence of our meagre historical documentation, and that of the tombstones, an earlier foundation for Lincoln in the later Claudian period (*c*.AD 47-54) remains a distinct possibility. The most contentious dating evidence takes the form of several legionary tombstones, most found in the nineteenth century in the lower part of town. These tombstones are evidence of occupation rather than campaigning, unless, that is, there was a temporary base here which needed to bury some of its dead before the fortress was founded. Experts on inscriptions have argued that the Ninth Legion tombstones lacking *cognomina* – the third or surname – (*RIB* 254, 255,

257: see further below) should be no later than *c.*AD 50 and thus indicate a legionary presence in the Claudian period, but there are later examples and the lack of *cognomina* cannot be taken to indicate such an early terminus. Lawrence Keppie suggests that they were just about universal by AD 69, but Lincoln's foundation was probably on the cusp of the change in practice.

Whatever conclusions are drawn on their date, the finding of early burials at a considerable distance of *c.*1–2km south of the hilltop fortress causes us to question seriously whether this could be the cemetery of the uphill fortress (**13**) or did it belong, perhaps, to an earlier fortress? There are certainly parallels for changing site, notably from Kingsholm to Gloucester – this one being of especial interest since the move, as that postulated at Lincoln, was previously linked with the risk of flooding and the position of the river crossing. It is now considered to relate to the presence

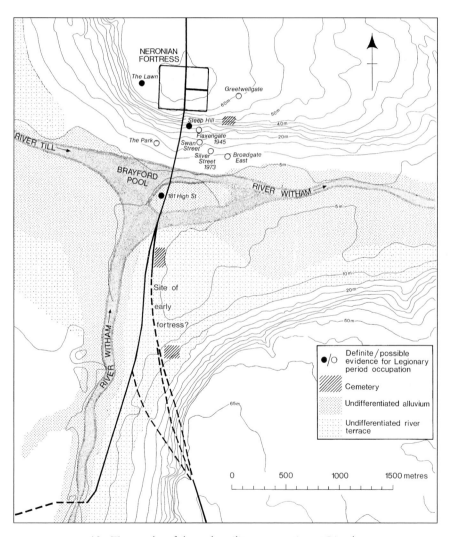

13 *Topography of the early military occupation at Lincoln*

of a native settlement. Could it be that the first base at Lincoln was similarly located on the 'friendly' south side of this settlement and the river? And might this base, although only containing part of the legion, have been from its inception the official headquarters of the Ninth, the only place where burial took place? Yet again the earliest pottery from the lower town area at Lincoln also appears to be no earlier than Neronian, and in view of the extent of damp ground it would still be quite acceptable for a cemetery at this distance to have served the uphill base (as at the permanent fortress at Caerleon, in South Wales, and Strasbourg, on the Rhine). Certainly the cemetery was still in use after the hilltop fortress was built.

There would have been little space for a full-sized fortress immediately north of the road junction – where it might be expected – and south of the marshy land in the St Marks area. This still leaves open the possibility of a base further south. Its site might have been on the gravel terraces east of the river, and aligned on to Ermine Street rather than the Fosse Way. As yet, however, there is no real evidence apart from the tombstones, and the discrepancies in dating, to corroborate this hypothesis. It is also conceivable that another base remains to be found elsewhere in the Lincoln area, even on the hilltop – where the construction camp was presumably located. Only further discoveries producing positive or negative evidence will advance our understanding.

The relationship to any native settlement here may have been an important factor in choosing where to base the garrison. Lincoln was accessible by road from the south and south-west, and by water from the south and south-east. On purely strategic grounds, however, the defensibility of a site with a steep scarp to the west as well as to the south could have proved decisive in the Roman army's selection of the hilltop site at Lincoln, even though the actual crossing of the river may have been easier a little further east (chapter 2). There were still difficulties with the site, which had to be accessed via a marshy valley and a steep climb to an area with poor water accessibility, but these were obviously considered secondary to other factors. Neither the low-lying land in the valley nor the steep, poorly draining hillside were options.

The reaction of the natives of the Witham basin to the arrival of the army is difficult to determine, but there must have been fears about the fate of any sites which were held in special esteem. The valley at Lincoln underwent great physical changes following the Conquest, with the construction of the new installations and linking roads. Traces of these changes survive but are hard to come by: deposits of the Roman military period are usually at the bottom of the sequence and, consequently, are quite fragmentary. Even so, surviving evidence from this period includes the buried remains of streets and (normally timber) buildings, well-preserved organic deposits in the waterlogged areas of the valley floor, and cremation burials. The army would in addition have taken control of a large area outside the fortress and in the surrounding countryside – its *territorium*. The existing state of knowledge of the fortress and its dependent settlement is set out in the next two chapters.

4 'Mediterraneans live here': the legionary fortress

The discovery of several tombstones in the late nineteenth and earlier twentieth centuries was the first decisive step forward in confirming the presence of legionaries at Lincoln (**14** & **colour plate 5**). The tombstones indicate successive garrisoning of a fortress first by the Ninth Legion *Hispana*, followed by the Second Legion *Adiutrix*, probably with the arrival back in Britain of the new governor Petilius Cerialis (former commander of the Ninth) in AD 71. The *origines* (places of origin) of the soldiers commemorated in the tombstones are of some interest: for the Ninth, the four known individuals, including the standard-bearer Caius Valerius, all came from regions close to the Mediterranean – Macedonia (northern Greece), Spain and Italy. It is probable that the legion had come to Britain from a base at Siscia (modern Sisak, Croatia), in the province of Pannonia, although confirmation is still awaited. After its residence at Lincoln, it went on to found the fortress at York in *c.*71, and it may have been at Carlisle temporarily later in the century. The Second *Adiutrix*, as its name ('supporting') implies, was a specially created force raised to supplement the existing army, and included ex-marines. One of its two documented members was from the important Gallic capital of Lyon; the other originated from Savaria, a colony on the Danubian frontier (now Hungary) in the province of Pannonia. This legion moved from Lincoln in 77-8 to build a new base at Chester.

Most of the tombstones were found in the area of Monson Street, off lower High Street (see below). The exceptions include one (or two) probably from north of the river, found incorporated into the rebuilt east wall of the Lower City, while Caius Valerius' stone (*RIB* 257) was found some distance south of Monson Street, towards the north end of South Common. The find on South Common was made in 1909 to the east of the railway; the stone may have been previously disturbed by the digging of the cutting in 1867. There were other definite finds of early cremations in this area in 1911 and 1981, so we can be confident that another part of the legionary cemetery lay so far to the south.

The fortress

Legionary fortresses had more or less evolved to a standard plan by the time Lincoln was constructed (**15**). Those that contained a whole legion of over 5,000 men

14 *Tombstone of Gaius Valerius, standard bearer of the Ninth Legion*

covered an area of 15-20ha (40-50 acres), and were rectangular in plan, normally squarish rather than elongated. Those built in the first century in Britain were almost wholly of timber, partly because time did not permit construction in stone of establishments which were only intended as interim bases. Each fortress was defended by an earthen rampart bank, with a vertical or near vertical front held in place by timber or clay/turf revetments respectively; timber fronts – as used at Lincoln – were less common in Britain, although normal in Germany. The rampart-walkway was fronted by a parapet, and towers were provided at regular intervals, at the angles, and at the four gateways. It was usual for legionary fortresses to have only one external ditch, whereas many smaller forts had two or even three.

Although the layout of the interior followed a fairly standard pattern, no two fortresses were identical. Their planning and architecture were similar in many ways to urban settlements, especially with regard to the principal streets, and some administrative structures, as well as the baths. One main street, the *via praetoria*, ran from the front gate (*porta praetoria*) to the entrance of the headquarters building (*principia*); to the rear it became the *via decumana*. The area in front of the other main street, the *via principalis*, linking two of the gates and running in front of the *principia*, was known as the *praetentura*. The *principia*, a forum-like complex with imperial statues in the courtyard, was the administrative and symbolic centre of the fortress: here the standards were kept in a central shrine in the range behind a cross-hall (*basilica principiorum*). The basilica, a large, aisled hall with a tribunal (platform) at one end, was used for addressing troops, for 'visible' administrative decisions, and for social gatherings. The standards were deliberately placed over the money chest containing pay and savings kept in a cellar, and they were guarded; theft constituted sacrilege. Weapons were stored in rooms either side of the courtyard.

To one side of the *principia* was the Commander's residence, the *praetorium*, of palatial dimensions and in the form of a Mediterranean peristyle house. Of the other most senior officers, the tribunes were of the highest rank, together with the *prae-fectus castrorum*, who was in charge of establishment. These all had houses of some pretension, in a line immediately in front of the *via principalis*. One of the six tribunes was of senatorial rather than equestrian rank, and would hope to achieve higher office in due course. Their space allocation was perhaps only a third of that occupied by the commander, but so deeply stratified was the Roman army that this was four or five times that given to a centurion and his staff, and in turn the ordinary soldier had only 2-3 per cent as much as the centurion. The soldiers were grouped in barrack blocks situated mainly adjacent to the street inside the rampart; each block was built to contain at least the 80 combatant troops in the century. The rest – those involved in administration, technical work, medical teams and cavalry troops – may have been housed in separate barracks. Normally, the barracks, in blocks of six, for each cohort, were subdivided into 10-14 *contubernia*, i.e. double rooms for sleeping and for equipment for up to eight men, with a verandah to the front. The centurion's apartment was normally at the rampart end, sometimes physically separated from the barracks, and it included some space for his office and assistants.

Other structures inside the fortress included the workshops (*fabrica*), for producing and repairing military equipment and everyday utensils, granaries (*horrea*) and stores, a hospital (*valetudinarium*), and communal baths. There were wells, water-channels (perhaps fed by an aqueduct), drains, and latrines to cover the needs of 5,000 men, and ovens for cooking, normally located against the internal face of the rampart. Immediately outside the enclosure might be found the parade-ground and the *ludus*, an amphitheatre used for training, and possibly also the establishments of those

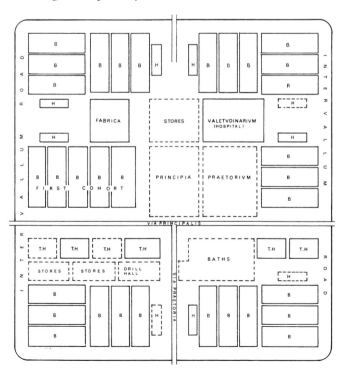

15 *Ideal layout of a legionary fortress.* From G. Webster (ed.) *Fortress into City*, 1988

craftsmen commissioned to produce goods for the garrison. The legion's use of the surrounding land did not stop there: they also took control of a swathe of land beyond.

The fortress' construction would have involved a good proportion of the legion for a matter of a few years, in addition to a large team supplying them with building materials and with food.

Lincoln's fortress

The principal clues to the fact that the uphill fortress underlay the *colonia* at Lincoln were the early coins, pottery and artefacts, some of military association, found when the prison inside the Castle was extended in 1846, during the construction of the Westgate reservoir in 1847-8, and in particular at the Water Tower built in 1910 (**colour plate 3**). The significance of these discoveries was not realised at the time, but as a result of excavations in the 1940s Graham Webster was able to confirm that the line of the fortress's northern and western defences lay beneath those of the *colonia*; Webster's investigations had fortuitously come across the legionary-period deposits very close to the modern ground surface (**6**). Hugh Thompson and Dennis Petch subsequently identified the eastern and southern lines. Apart from remains of structures adjacent to the rampart, little progress could, however, be reported in elucidating the internal arrangements: generally the fortress' slight remains are deeply buried, difficult to investigate and in places already destroyed. Only slight hints of early buildings were noted during work on the *colonia* baths, a site which yielded much early pottery – presumably from rubbish pits and demolition deposits of the fortress structures. The fortress baths could not have covered quite the same area: legionary baths did not necessarily occupy the same locations; at Exeter, their site became that of the civic forum. The position of the *colonia* baths at Lincoln is, however, similar to those at the Ninth Legion's fortress at York, and those at Caerleon, but those of the fortress might alternatively be situated in the range to the rear of the *principia*.

The space available inside the defences measured *c*.440m east-west by *c*.360m north-south, perhaps 1,500 by 1,200 Roman feet (**16**), a layout based on standard units of 50 or 100 Roman feet. The scheme here allows for barrack blocks, plus the width of an adjacent street, to measure up to 300 Roman feet – although many contemporary examples were shorter. Eight of the ten cohorts could be accommodated to the north and south of the *via praetoria* and *via decumana* in the blocks closest to both east and west gates. The first cohort would normally occupy some of the area to the south of the *principia*, and possibly some of the space to the north of it, fronting on to the *via principalis*. There would then still be room for the final, tenth cohort. But the arrangement could be more complex, as known from Exeter, where the barracks were shorter in length. It is likely that in these early years of the conquest the garrisoning of all bases had to be flexible.

The identification of the *principia* (see below) demonstrated that the *via principalis* ran north-south (roughly along the line of modern Bailgate/upper Steep Hill), and confirmed that the fortress gates would have underlain those of the *colonia*. The

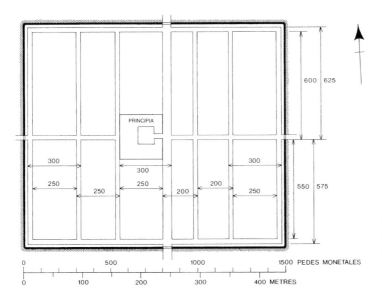

16 *Theoretical layout of the fortress street system at Lincoln, using standard units of measurement*

remains of the east gate excavated in 1963-6, a tower based on nine large posts, would then represent those of the *porta praetoria*, the front gate. Certainly this entrance was a double carriageway, while that to the rear of the *principia*, the *porta decumana* (west gate), was certainly only a single carriageway wide in the succeeding *colonia* period. We can establish little else of the internal layout. The area of the fortress, at *c*.15ha (or *c*.40 acres) is only *c*.80 per cent of the normal size found later, but it is difficult to know if a full legion or only part was housed here, since none of the barrack blocks has been investigated to any large extent – it may be rather that the barracks were shorter or there were fewer ancillary buildings. It seems probable that the fortifications and the streets were dealt with early in the construction process, while the soldiers were in temporary accommodation, either within the area of the fortress, or outside it: evidence of early structures to the west of the enclosure might represent an earlier base rather than extra-mural occupation contemporary with the fortress.

The streets were presumably set out and surfaced early in the process in order to facilitate building work. There is unfortunately little information on the legionary streets. The *intervallum* road inside the rampart, the *via sagularis*, was noted on the south side at the Sub-deanery in 1955-8, on the north side in the 1940s, and its line at least located further east at East Bight in 1980. Here it was *c*.5-6m wide, perhaps nominally 20 Roman feet.

The nature of the legionary fortifications has been elucidated during a series of excavations (**17**). A rampart bank, 10 Roman feet wide, was formed of the clayey material dug from the ditch and founded on a 'corduroy' of split timbers to create friction and minimise slip. It was fronted by timber planking held in place by uprights set 5 Roman feet apart. It is possible that a turf or clay revetment may have been intended originally: the use of timber fronts was comparatively rare in Britain and its occurrence at Lincoln might best be explained by the unsuitably loose nature of the earth. Alternatively, the engineer or camp prefect who ordered its construction had previous experience of the timber fronts standard in the Rhineland. As was normal for fortresses, only a single ditch, *c.*15 Roman feet wide by 6 feet deep, was provided. At least one tower projecting beyond the original line was added subsequently, and if part of a general scheme this would probably have meant digging a new ditch further out. Traces of so-called 'rampart-buildings', in some cases 'cookhouses' (possibly bread-ovens) appeared between the rampart and the *via sagularis* on the line of the northern defences, at North Row – evidenced here by waste dumps – and at East Bight. Metalworking refuse and copper-alloy fragments from associated deposits adjacent to the East Bight structures may have been derived from a workshop undertaking repairs to armour and equipment.

Where the excavation trenches extended inside the *via sagularis*, the fringes of the adjacent buildings, presumably barracks, were revealed. At Westgate, three rooms of a block were identified running east-west, and were presumably therefore remains of the centurion's quarters – although the function of each individual room is unclear. Some good quality glass of first-century date came from this site, reflecting something of the centurion's material lifestyle. The military demolition dump contained early pottery as well as many fragments of military equipment, including objects associated with cavalry. The most notable object was a dagger scabbard, with decorated panels of silver inlay, possibly therefore the property of a centurion (**colour plate 15**).

Fragments of other fortress structures at Chapel Lane (1985) included two successive phases of timber buildings, with different internal arrangements; both may still have been barracks. Close to Chapel Lane, at West Bight in 1976, the demolition debris beneath the make-up for a *colonia*-period building included some wattle and daub, rendered prior to being given a plaster surface.

With the exception of the *principia*, the constructional details of the legionary fortress buildings at Lincoln appear to indicate two different types of construction, continuous wall-trenches and intermittent post-holes, possibly indicating different functions, and white-painted wattle and daub walls. Several sites show traces of rebuilding, while repairs to the rampart's timber front were noted in several places. Evidence of the demolition of buildings, in some places involving fires, at or after the end of the fortress' life is convincing.

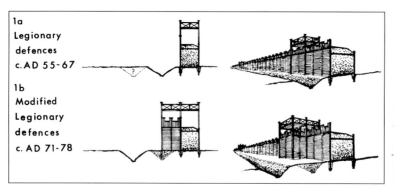

1a
Legionary
defences
c. AD 55-67

1b
Modified
Legionary
defences
c. AD 71-78

17 *Reconstruction drawing of the two phases of the legionary fortifications, with approximate dates.* D. Vale

18 *Post-pit for one of the large posts of the*
principia *cross hall, showing shape of the*
actual post

19 *General view of the* principia
excavations, 1978, showing the large
post-pits of the cross-hall, left; looking
north-east

The *principia*

The remains of the *principia* revealed in 1978-9 took the form of both post-pits, for posts 12 by 8 Roman inches in section, and post-holes, some of which were linked by wall-trenches, as well as areas of external pebble surfaces (**18** & **19**); no internal floors survived. Two phases of construction were again discovered, suggesting a remodelling of the timber cross-hall (*basilica principiorum*), possibly to meet the requirements of the incoming legionary commander wishing to impose his mark. The area covered by the investigations measured almost 50m east-west, from the nave of the cross-hall to the inner wall of the east range fronting on to the *via principalis*. There were remains suggestive of a water-supply: a timber-lined channel, or long tank, within the basilica, and stone bases for water storage-tanks or basins in the courtyard, served perhaps by the well later capped in the *colonia* period (see below). The presence of the well towards the corner of the *principia* courtyard is mirrored in a number of other major forts: water was also required for religious ceremonies.

Although fragmentary, the plan indicated a hall to the west of a courtyard, which was clearly the *principia* (**20**). It measured 50-75m north-south and *c.*70m east-west, and its courtyard extended *c.*30m (*c.*100 Roman feet) east-west. The layout can be compared most closely with two earlier German examples: that at Haltern (the 'Hauptlager'), on the river Lippe, and the more recently discovered *principia* at Marktbreit. Both were occupied only for a short period, but with sufficient time at

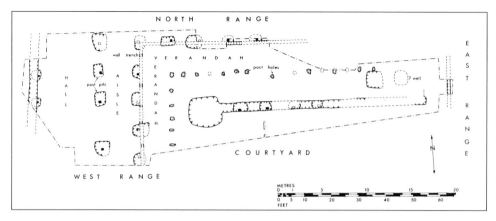

20 *Plan of the features of the* principia *excavated 1978-9. The east-west trench may have been dug to bring water from the well to a tank in the courtyard*

Haltern for major building alterations. There is some merit in comparing the Lincoln *principia* with that at Longthorpe, where a range only 1.83m wide was provided to the rear. It is notable that at neither Longthorpe nor Haltern were any remains found of verandah posts, or water channels: either they were not provided, or possibly the evidence was too slight to be noted by the excavators.

As has been noted, alterations to the *principia* were made whilst the site was under military control, and it is presumed that this happened before the site was handed over to the civilian authority. The rebuilding may well have been occasioned by the poor physical state of the structure: whether this was the case or not, the arrival of the Second *Adiutrix* would provide one possible context. The fact that the Lincoln example resembled those in Augustan Germany, built *c.*50 years earlier, might point to the use of manuals containing blueprints, and hence some conservatism in military design, rather than to particular legions or their responsible engineers, but some individual choice is apparent.

The *principia* courtyard was kept fairly clean; few artefacts were recovered to provide close dating of its construction or use. The pottery can only be assigned to the Neronian and early Flavian periods (*c.*AD 55-*c.*AD 80), and there were no coins stratified in these earliest deposits. The site did produce coins pre-dating the Conquest of Mark Antony and Augustus/Tiberius, no doubt brought over with the legion.

5 Occupation outside the fortress

The amount which the army required in terms of equipment, animals and food was enormous, and explains why fortresses were situated close to navigable rivers. The legion had its own workshops: it contained soldiers skilled in various tasks, such as making and repairing materials and armour. But some services and goods could only be provided from outside the fortress – food stuffs, and raw materials for building and industrial processes. The extent to which equipment was manufactured by the legion, and how much was obtained from external sources, remains uncertain. Some provisions were, of course, obtained locally.

The soldiers also had time and money for social activity, some of which was expended in the settlement outside the fortress. The traders' booths (*canabae*) were leased out by fixed-term agreements and usually lined the street outside one or more of the gates. The inhabitants of the civilian settlements might have included traders and artisans such as potters, both local and immigrant, but also soldiers' sexual partners (they were not allowed to marry at this time) and their families and, in time, veterans from the legion. Taverns offered scope for contacts between soldier and civilian. They were still military property so buildings that had encroached too closely could be demolished. Beyond the *canabae*, the next element was normally the cemetery (including civilian graves). The civil settlement (*vicus*), further out, could, however, become quite extensive, and areas could still be under military control even at considerable distance from the fortress.

The spread of the settlement was controlled by the military authorities, and particular areas zoned for the army's needs, including some river frontage for warehouses. A further requirement was space for compounds and grazing land for draught animals and the cavalry's horses. An amphitheatre or *ludus* (training ground) would have been normal; the most likely location was on level ground outside one of the gates. Beyond the built-up area were the *prata* ('meadows') of the legion, discussed below, part of the *territorium* taken under control. The demands of the army's presence thus placed something of a burden on the local populace, but also offered opportunities: no doubt it also acted as a stimulus to economic activity, attracting traders and artisans.

At Lincoln, the army controlled a large area surrounding its fortress (**21**), and beyond the river to the south, including the cemetery (**13** & **22**). Evidence for settlement outside the west gate of the fortress is provided by large amounts of pottery and glass of mid- to late first-century date and by military artefacts, including horse-trappings. It is difficult to know on present evidence if this material was derived from actual military occupation, such as an early fort or labour camp,

21 *Artist's reconstruction of the fortress on the hilltop. The amphitheatre-like structure* (ludus) *to the right of the fortress is conjectural.* D. Vale

or an annexe, rather than from the activities of resident traders. Among the pottery was a native-style beaker of a type originating in north Buckinghamshire or Northamptonshire, presumably brought here by a legionary who moved with his garrison from that area. To the north and east of the fortress, there have been few investigations close to the gates, but it is likely that these areas were also intensively used. About 600m north of the north gate, first-century high-status pottery discovered in excavations indicates contemporary occupation nearby, most likely to represent natives producing for the army, perhaps drawn to the line of the road from another nearby location. It is possible that part of the *canabae*, and perhaps burial grounds and a *ludus* lay in this uphill area with its level ground, but nearer to the fortress. An extensive surface *c.*200m east of the east gate laid on the natural cornbrash is difficult to interpret, especially in the absence of dating evidence, but could have belonged to a parade ground or even the *ludus*. The most likely location for the amphitheatre-like *ludus* was outside, north of the back gate, the *porta decumana*, west of the fortress, although no structural remains have come to light. Later use of this area might point to a major earthwork, levelled together with part of the Roman rampart hereabouts: this problem is discussed in more detail below.

The inclusion of the lower city (later walled) in the succeeding *colonia* makes it reasonable to presume that at least some of the *canabae* lay on the hillside to the south of the fortress. Few excavations have in fact reached the earliest deposits; timber

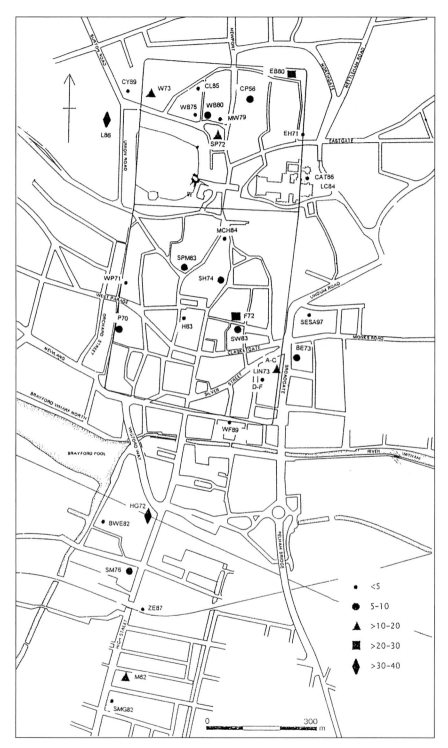

22 *Distribution of early military finds from excavations 1970-90, showing concentrations also outside the fortress*

structures to the east of Ermine Street were noted in 1974 on a site which produced samian pottery and some early glass (**22**). Legionary-period occupation would be expected adjacent to the main north-south route if anywhere, but excavations further east, at the east end of Silver Street and east of Broadgate, also produced much early pottery. A later Roman dock wall (discussed below) was noted to the south and may have been located on the line of an early river inlet. Several other sites on the hillside have yielded first-century pottery and other artefacts, residual in later contexts, particularly dating to the decade AD 70-80. These objects might have originated from nearby *canabae* structures: one notable find was a Rhodian *amphora* from a site near to the bottom of Spring Hill.

Beyond the river

Excavations south of the river have actually produced most stratified material associated with extra-mural occupation during the legionary period (**22**). At the site of 181-3 High Street, which overlay native structures built on a sand 'island', the artefactual evidence – including a spearhead (**colour plate 16**) – and a small collection of animal bones announce the arrival of the new Roman occupants. At least one long structure, with painted walls, dates to the legionary period. Its street-front site could indicate a commercial function, although a directly military use cannot be ruled out. To its south was a southern course of the river, crossed by a causeway, at least some of which is likely to have been constructed by the army. South of this marshy land the routes to London (Ermine Street) and to Leicester and the south-west (Fosse Way) diverged, in the vicinity of modern King Street (**13**).

Cemeteries

The discovery of cremation burials at Monson Street in 1982 confirmed the impression given by nineteenth-century finds of legionary tombstones and other early records, that this was indeed the site of an early cemetery. The graves had been made by shallow scoops into the sand, and were located by grave-markers set into slots in the ground. The containers, including pottery vessels, held cremated remains. The burial rite had distinctively Roman elements rather than native. It is now possible to date and sex cremated bone: of those individuals found (at least four in number), only one could have been a soldier, the others being women or children. The inscribed memorials demonstrate that soldiers were being buried here, but there were also civilians, perhaps the legionaries' 'wives' and their children or those of traders. Animal bones, a common phenomenon in Romano-British graves, probably represented sacrificial meals. Other artefacts which had survived the cremation process included hobnails, and glass containers (*unguentaria*) for anointing the corpse with oil or perfume (**colour plate 7**). The vessels had normally been placed on the pyre, since most had melted. A mirror, an item of grave furniture known in the Late Iron

Age, is a further indicator that some had access to valuable objects. A stone building adjacent might be interpreted as a mausoleum for someone of even greater distinction, although no burials were found in the fragment of it excavated. A nineteenth-century note of a nearby discovery also mentioned an area of charcoal and soot, perhaps the *ustrina*, or pyre-site.

Other burials are known further south, among them the tombstone of the legionary Gaius Saufeius. That of the standard-bearer Caius Valerius came from South Common several hundred metres beyond (**14**). Both belonged to the Ninth Legion. South Common has also produced two other cremations, both closer to the projected line of Ermine Street than that of the Fosse Way, but at least one belongs to the early *colonia* period. The general picture appears to be that land south of the river crossing was designated as cemetery. The most southerly cemetery does not appear to have continued in use beyond the second century.

There may have been other legionary cemeteries. A tombstone found incorporated into the rebuilt city wall north of the lower east gate might be evidence that the hillside south-east of the fortress was used for burial: cremations have been found in that area.

The military road system

Outside the fortress, some of the routes are known, but the evidence for constructional detail is poor. The steepness of the slope to the river was such that wheeled vehicles probably had to follow a diagonal route, as in the *colonia* period. In the valley, the location of the junction between Ermine Street and the Fosse Way was determined by the extent of marshy ground. Some form of causeway connecting the island to higher ground would have been necessary. In 1877-8, the engineer Michael Drury noted a causeway in a number of locations, and of two apparent phases: a layer of 'concrete' above a 'muddy' layer. The concrete layer was less substantial where there was a higher sand terrace (**2**). Drury also noted that the causeway led to a wooden ramp further north based on timber piles, while excavations in 1989 suggested that there could also have been a ford adjacent to the east. It seems most likely that the 'muddy' layer represents an embankment built by the army leading to a timber bridge over the river.

The exact routes of the Fosse Way and Ermine Street beyond are still problematic. The probable line of Ermine Street diverging from the Fosse Way was discovered in 1982, and aerial photographs suggesting its line beyond make it likely that it ran east of the modern line, directly across the line of South Common close to the early burial finds here. The Fosse Way's crossing of the Witham may have taken place a little further south of the existing bridge at Bracebridge, before adopting the line of its route south-westwards to Leicester. Its route beyond linked a series of Roman forts in a straight line (already mentioned above). All may have had pre-Roman origins, but perhaps not directly adjacent to the road line. Along Ermine Street to the south, the presumed fort at Navenby (on the evidence of artefacts) and that at Ancaster, where structural remains have been found, policed existing native settlements (**12** & **60**). To the north of Lincoln there is a similar pattern of settlements *c*.10 Roman miles apart, with the same sequence likely of native centre, fort, and civilian settlement, at Owmby, Hibaldstow, and Winteringham on the south bank of the Humber. Ermine Street ran straight for the first 38km, before diverting slightly to the west for the route to the Humber crossing. Experts disagree about the methods used to survey the route.

The legion's territory

Outside the area of the fortress and related settlement, but somewhere within the territory taken over by the army, were the *prata legionis* ('meadows'), used for stock grazing and related activities. Areas of pasture were needed to graze horses, cattle and sheep, and woodland areas for building materials and fuel. The area covered could well have been extensive but there is no evidence as yet for its location or extent at Lincoln, and it will be extremely difficult to define it. The legionary territory may have occupied much of the same land as that of the later *colonia*, but would presumably have been related to the land required to feed the troops, unless, as has been shown at York, some of the grain was imported.

Clues to the extent of the territory might be provided by the existence of practice-camps, outlying sources of water serving the fortress, and demolition of features potentially useful to hostile natives: the triple ditch-system east of Lincoln is a good example of the last. Iron Age rural settlements continuing into the Roman period might have lain outside the formal territory, and on present indications the nearest of these lies *c*.8km from the fortress site. Some recently-discovered settlements on the edge of the Witham Valley *c*.20km south-east of Lincoln have produced high-status imported pottery, perhaps indicating that they were manufacturing for the army, or belonged to a social group which was able to afford such items.

6 Colony: the foundation of a city

Transition: fortress to city

By the mid-70s, a generation had passed since the army had first appeared in the region, and there was sufficient confidence to remove direct military control as the conquest of Britain again moved up a gear. When *Legio II Adiutrix* departed to Chester in the late 70s AD, the fortress became a shell of its former self. Its buildings were dismantled; perhaps some timbers were rescued for re-use, but others were burned. Excavations have shown that some of the posts of the *principia* cross-hall were sawn off, but most were actually withdrawn. Only the fortifications were definitely left in position, for security and to indicate that the site was still under official control. The traditional view is that a caretaker garrison remained in place to oversee the demolition and to keep an eye on the local population. The withdrawal of the troops must have had an impact on those who had depended on them for their living, and some may have moved on with the military advance. Certainly, the amount of pottery from excavations falls in the last two decades of the century, and may reflect the temporary downturn in economic activity.

The subsequent decision to create a military colony required the emperor's endorsement. A *colonia* was the highest status awarded to provincial cities, and it was frequently used in this period for settlements of retired legionaries, who already had the required Roman citizenship. It was an expedient choice: the land was already under official control, with an infrastructure in place. Its selection as a *colonia* may have owed much to its distance from Leicester (over 80km to the south-west), which became the official tribal capital of the Corieltauvi at the expense of Old Sleaford, perhaps on spatial grounds. Lincoln's designation may also have been connected with the increasing need for a new colony to accommodate legionary veterans. It was shortly to be followed by Gloucester, while the fortresses at Exeter and Wroxeter became tribal capitals. The veteran colonies would have a political value in other ways, in the collection of taxes, as models of urbanised culture, and in due course as a source of legionary recruits.

A clue to the foundation date of *Colonia Domitiana Lindensium* – its probable formal name – is provided by the inscribed stone at Mainz dedicated by a citizen of Lincoln origin. He was Marcus Minicius Marcellinus, a retired chief centurion in *Legio XXII Primigenia*, and another potential member of *Lindum's* founding civic elite – had he ever returned. The inscription (*CIL*, 13, 6679) can be dated to the Flavian period (AD 69-96) (**23**). It has been generally assumed that the colony would not have been established until after *c.*AD 86, because of the army's pre-occupation in

23 *Dedication stone set up to Fortuna by Marcus Minicius Marcellinus, a citizen of the colony of Lincoln before AD 96.* Found in Mainz, Germany

campaigns in Wales and northern Britain until that date, but there is no certainty on this point. The foundation of Gloucester (probably under the Emperor Nerva, 96-8) may be seen as continuing the same strategy, but possibly more than a decade after Lincoln. The veterans who constituted the original colonists were probably several hundred strong, if not more, and from more than one legion.

The new city was given a legal charter. Surviving examples from some earlier Spanish colonies provide some idea of the local administrative arrangements, based on a council (*ordo*), possibly of 100 councillors (decurions). Selection for the *ordo* would involve meeting social and financial criteria, and they were normally required to maintain a house in or near to the *colonia*, or at least in the *territorium*, which was also covered by the town's charter. Lincoln can boast a rare example of a tombstone set up by a decurion, Aurelius Senecio. The stone probably dates to the third century, but his wife, Volusia Faustina, may have been descended from a veteran settler (*RIB* 250) (**24**). Of the dual magistrates elected annually by the council, the *duoviri* were responsibile for legal and other matters, the *aediles* for public services, and there may also have been *quaestores*, in charge of public finances. The Imperial Cult was in the hands of the priests known as the *seviri augustales*, often successful traders who had formerly been slaves and as such did not qualify for higher office. Two are known from Lincoln: a probable wine-merchant, Marcus Aurelius Lunaris (AD 237), with similar responsibilities in York (**colour plate 10**), and the benefactor who rebuilt a temple – presumably that of the Imperial cult – in gratitude for his election. Expenditure of this sort was expected from holders of the post.

The settlers
Former soldiers of the Ninth Legion (now based in York) probably formed a major element of the new colonial population, perhaps together with others who had

24 *Tombstone of Volusia Faustina, aged 26, set up by her husband Aurelius Senecio, a town councillor* (decurio). British Museum

fought in the Northern campaigns. On the evidence of discharge certificates, it is clear that most ex-soldiers preferred to spend their retirement in the provinces in which they had served and where they might have developed long-term relationships. They were rewarded with land and/or a cash grant. Those being discharged at Lincoln, following 25 years' service, had been recruited in the 60s and early 70s, the later ones including many non-Italians. These were ex-soldiers, and cannot therefore be presumed to have represented in general the most 'civilised' of the Empire's citizens. Yet the extent to which they had experienced Mediterranean culture early in their lives could well have influenced their preferences in terms of architecture and other materials, including diet, which may be apparent in the archaeological record. The evidence in general for Romano-British towns indicates that the mature *coloniae* differed little from the *civitas* capitals in terms of economy and diet. Yet this partial loss of distinctiveness is what might be expected by the third century. The earlier colonial phases may have been more distinctively Mediterranean in this respect, but it is difficult to know to what extent there was also a native element (*incolae*) in the population of the original city.

The upper city: symbols of power

The new *colonia* developed a Roman urban identity in its first half-century: the timber fortress was replaced by a stone city, facilitated by the fact that it stood on a source of good building stone. During the first half of the second century a stone front was added to the earth and timber rampart, and a range of impressive public buildings rose, supported by a new infrastructure of roads, water supply and drains. This was a period of heavy investment on public works in the cities of Roman Britain. The various undertakings swallowed huge amounts of resources, most probably paid for by the authorities, but their remains still on the whole lie buried under the modern city. Ian Richmond wrote in 1946: 'The tale of structures within the *colonia* is thus a sorry one. All too many opportunities have been missed.' Until 1957, none was investigated on any scale, and since then only the public baths and the forum have been identified, but are still imperfectly understood.

The street system (25)

The streets provided a means whereby the materials of the new architecture and services could be physically introduced, as well as providing a formal setting for their realisation. Excavations in the 1970s made it clear that, contrary to earlier views, the layout of the Roman town was no longer discernible in the present layout: apart from the northern part of the main north-south street (roughly followed here by Bailgate), the Roman grid had been lost in the post-Roman period. Nor had it been imposed *de novo*, as if on a greenfield site; rather, the city's plan was based on that of the fortress. Some military streets may have been resurfaced, and reconstruction of existing roads accommodated a new drainage system. In other cases, the earlier streets were abandoned and sealed by new buildings. Richmond pointed out the potential of the Roman sewers for understanding the street pattern, but probably underestimated the practical difficulties of following their course – there has been little progress.

Our knowledge of the street system has been growing for over a century. In 1888, Michael Drury noted the principal north-south street (the *cardo*) in the Bailgate area, at a width of *c.*27 feet (*c.*8.3m). The contemporary discovery of the Bailgate colonnade established that the width of the entrance into the forum, on the line of the street (the *decumanus*) linking the east and west gates, was *c.*15-16 feet wide (*c.*4.5-4.8m – the column-centres being *c.*6m apart). Along the colonnaded east frontage of the forum the street was much wider if the wide porticoes are included, and the north and south gateways were in all at least 40 Roman feet wide.

Less significant routes were narrower. The gap south of the forum colonnade, presumably that of a further street, was *c.*17 feet (*c.*5m) wide. To the north of the colonnade, a new east-west street (found in 1980) was built adjacent to the Mint Wall following its construction at or soon after the end of the second century; it measured at least 5m wide, but probably not much more. An earlier street running parallel with and to the west of the *cardo* at Chapel Lane was at least *c.*4-5m wide. It was only in use for a short while. The excavations of the public baths at Cottesford Place revealed

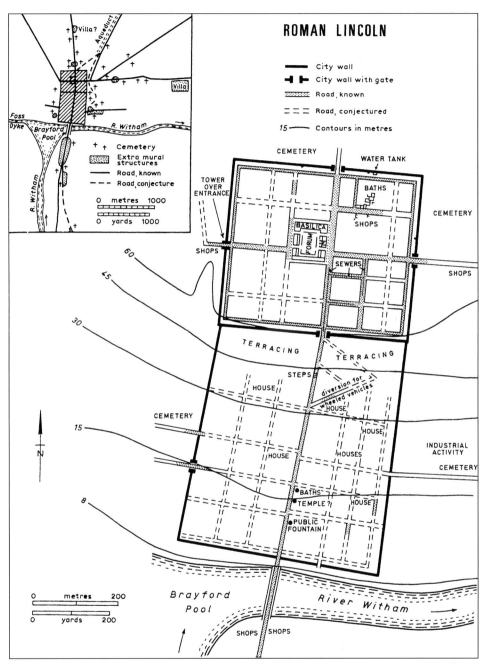

25 *Plan of the Roman city, with (inset) the extent of the cemeteries and suburbs*

a further major east-west street, up to 10m wide in places but narrower elsewhere, leading eastwards from the *cardo* to the south of the baths. A narrow north-south lane, perhaps of military origin, *c*.4m (13ft) wide, joined it to the street inside the fortifications, but was later built over as the baths were extended westwards. The intervallum road inside the rampart has itself been excavated on the north and south sides. These were later resurfaced, having widths not exceeding *c*.6m (20ft), with indications of a narrow foot way adjacent to the structures inside the street (**26**). The road can also be presumed on the east and west sides.

Most of the street surfaces appear to have been formed of small pebbles, but the principal north-south street, as noted most recently in a small trench in Bailgate 1997, was paved with large blocks. This evidence corroborates that from records of the road adjacent to the Bailgate colonnade, and that from Michaelgate on the hillside to the south. The principal east-west street may have been given the same treatment, which does not appear to have extended beyond the gates apart from the line of Ermine Street in the Lower City.

Evidence for the street layout also indicates that the known blocks (*insulae*) of the *colonia* varied in size and shape. This irregularity probably stems from the fact that some of the streets of the fortress were retained, while others were replaced. The plan (**25**) identifies what is known.

Water supply and drainage

A large sewer was found beneath the main north-south street at roughly the same time as the colonnade was emerging in Bailgate, and feeders into the system were also discovered. The main drain was all of 1.4m (4ft 6in) high – sufficient for inspection and cleaning (**27**). A 15m-long section was traced in 1838, and a much longer section in 1883, but modern access and investigation have not been able to determine either

26 *Road inside northern rampart at East Bight, 1981, looking north. The adjacent stone house is visible in the foreground, with a footway just beyond. The stones top left may belong to a ramp created to heighten the city wall*

27 *Engraving of the main sewer with side-channels*

its structure or what its fills might contain in the way of artefactual and environmental evidence. A possible extension continuing down the hillside was revealed in 1986, and although no further evidence has been recovered, it probably went all the way to the river. Surface- and storm-water drains were noted beneath some of the side streets. That situated at Cottesford Place may also have carried the outflow from the public baths, and was stone-lined. The new drain at East Bight had stone sides and a slab cover, but its base was an elliptical channel cut into the clay: this was designed to ensure a constant velocity of flow in order to minimise silting (**28**).

Further west on East Bight, excavations revealed a structure *c*.16m (*c*.55ft) long built at the rear of the city wall in the early second century. It was a water tank (*castellum aquae*), based on a rubble foundation *c*.5m deep, and lined with Roman waterproof 'concrete' (*opus signinum*) (**29**). It may have been vaulted, and its capacity has been estimated at *c*.12,000 litres. Its purpose was to store and distribute water supplied from the aqueduct. The construction of the aqueduct, the baths and the sewers in turn was probably conceived as an integrated scheme. The water tank

28 *Drain found at East Bight in 1981*

29 *Reconstruction of the upper city looking south-west towards the water tank just beyond the city wall and public baths nearby.*
D. Vale

served the public baths, and perhaps the public fountain in the lower city (unless there was another pipeline), and in turn to flush out the sewers. When sufficient water was available, it might also provide water to private houses. There may have been other aqueducts and tanks: the sewers would imply that a large volume of water was available, rather than just relying on rainwater. The known pipeline built to bring water into the city from the north/north-east could not have supplied the whole city: some of the city's water supply would have come from wells, including that in the east range of the forum (see below), whose capacity was *c.*13,500 litres. The aqueduct itself is discussed within the section on extra-mural occupation, below.

Fortifications

The defensive sequence of the Upper City has been much studied, all four sides of the circuit having been the subject of excavations, and some elements still survive above ground, although ruinous. The walls and ditches were subject to regular repair, but some major programmes are discernible, each probably taking decades to achieve. The walls followed the line of the fortress, whose rampart was left in position and formed a useful basis, as at Gloucester: the *coloniae* were the only towns to receive imperial permission to build stone fortifications in Britain before the later second century. Use of stone at the same time implied consolidation and was an expression by the urban community of its status. Analysis of the sources of materials and methods of construction suggested that the better beds of limestone were not used at first, at least for the city wall: perhaps they had not been identified.

Construction began in the early second century. After the new stone front was built in front of the legionary rampart, the earlier timber revetment was removed and material dumped into the gap. The wall, *c.*1.2m (4ft) wide and standing *c.*4m high, was surrounded by a ditch that had to be newly dug, since the stone front extended over the former legionary ditch. A system of interval towers, *c.*5m by 6m externally and about 40m apart, was added to the inner face of the wall at some later date.

There were about forty in all. In the late second or early third century, the rampart and wall were heightened, the wall's height being raised to *c.*6m. Another major rebuilding took place in the late third or fourth century. This saw a considerable thickening and heightening of the wall, now standing *c.*7-8m – and of the rampart bank, as well as the digging of a much wider ditch, measuring *c.*25m across; its combined width with the defensive barrier was a formidable 40m or so. At East Bight the late rampart had extended over the intervallum road, which must have gone out of use during the fourth century. Some of the dumps of material found on the rampart represented rubbish from the internal buildings.

Gates

Lincoln's Roman gates are justly famous, on account of both their good survival and their investigation. The four gates of the fortress were all replaced in stone. Although initially this consisted merely of a frontal cladding, in the third century they developed into monumental structures. They became important symbols, with entrances flanked by tall towers. The most well-known is the north gate (Newport Arch, **30**), since its rear arches are still standing and the front of its west tower has also been uncovered. In plan, it consisted of a single carriageway flanked by two pedestrian arches. The semi-circular fronted towers had chamfered bases. In this detail it resembled the east gate, which was formerly the *porta praetoria* (front gate) of the legionary fortress, and which preserved the double carriageway from that period. Its monumental towers were dated by excavation to the early part of the third century. They display horizontal marks made with a claw-chisel, and other traces of the masons' tools. The 'back' gate (the west) was exposed by accident in 1836 to the

30 *Newport Arch, internal face of the north gate, looking north*

astonishment of those who witnessed the event (see cover). It was depicted sufficiently for its plan to be largely understood, but has been little explored since. It was a smaller structure, a tower with a single carriageway beneath.

The south gate has been the most problematic of the four, partly because of the confusing nature of the antiquarian accounts. The springing of a carriageway arch was visible on Steep Hill into the late eighteenth century. In the building to the east, Thomas Sympson had noted in 1737 the existence of an 'east postern, 7 foot in diameter', suggesting a side passage as at the north gate, but a drawing of roughly the same date by Nathan Drake (which only came to light in 1983) suggested a second carriageway of greater dimensions than a pedestrian arch. A further confusing piece of evidence is a sketch by Grimm of the remains of the gate-arches which depicts both a double carriageway and the edge of a side passage, and another early description also gives this impression. How do we reconcile these various accounts? The question of whether the gate had one or two carriageways seemed destined not to be resolved, but refurbishment of number 44 Steep Hill in 2001 has revealed not only the large blocks of the east wall of the eastern carriageway, but also the two lowest stones of the *spina*, the wall between the two arches. It now seems likely that Sympson was perhaps describing only what was visible in the upper floor – the narrow top of the arch.

A double carriageway is therefore confirmed, but the question still remains as to whether it also had pedestrian side passages (**31**). This question is compounded by the existence of an undated curving wall on the west side of Steep Hill, i.e. to the west of the western carriageway. If part of a circular or part-circular tower, there

31 *Reconstruction drawing of the South Gate. The side passages are only speculative.* D. Vale

would not be sufficient room for a western postern. There is no evidence for a similar feature on the east side, but circular drum-towers, of various sizes and designs, were attached to Roman gates at several sites on the Rhine-Danube frontier and towns in Northern Italy. The south-east gate (*porta leoni*) at Verona had square towers which were circular internally. This may help explain the remains at Lincoln, or it is possible that the curving wall may merely have formed part of a quadrant to the rear of the wall-line.

In any case, the south gate was a monumental structure, with at least two carriageways. We must leave open for the moment the question of side-passages, but the same plan is known at Colchester, Verulamium and Silchester.

Public buildings

In addition to the provision of public works, the new *colonia* also boasted a wide range of public monuments. There are traces of several major buildings, but only the forum, overlying the legionary *principia* at the junction of the main streets, and the baths, in the north-eastern sector, have been definitely identified so far. Of other apparently major structures we have but glimpses: a colonnade to the north of the Cathedral; another structure with engaged columns further west, fronting on to the main north-south street; a brick-colonnaded building on the same frontage, to the east and north of the forum; and solid walls and floors indicative of public monuments to the west and the south of the forum. Taken together, they suggest the presence of several major structures along the two main streets of the city.

The civic centre: forum and basilica

The forum was the central and, symbolically, the most important building of the *colonia*. It did not consist of a single structure, but of several, each with a different function, grouped around a square. It was both a public space and a religious centre, and normally where civic functions were concentrated. In its most complete form, it consisted of various components: the square (often lined with porticoes), a temple, a hall (*basilica*) with attached administrative offices, and a council chamber (*curia*). In Gaul and other provinces, the complex was often of the so-called 'double-precinct' or 'tripartite' type, with a temple precinct facing across the forum to the basilica. In Britain, however, the so-called 'principia-type' of forum was common (although not universal), with temples usually forming a separate structure. Gloucester's forum was of the second type, echoing the plan of the legionary *principia* directly beneath. The decision to adopt this plan was not necessarily the result of using military architects: there were continuing mutual influences between military and civilian designs. At the same time, ex-army engineers were likely to have been available for technical advice to the new towns. There were also great differences in scale between the fora of Britain, possibly related to the size of the town and its population. Prosperity, or pretension, may have been better represented by quality and finish than by size.

The identification of the remains of the forum at Lincoln has had a long and fascinating history. The finding of tessellated floors in areas several metres to the west of the Bailgate colonnade, where a courtyard surface might have been expected, led Ian

Richmond to conclude that the colonnade and related nearby structures could not be interpreted as either a forum or a basilica. Rather, he suggested a series of three adjacent buildings, including at least one temple. This went to some extent against the views of George Fox, who had set out the plan of the colonnade in 1892, proposing that the basilica was at its northern end, and that the forum lay across the street to the east (**32**); and also contradicted Tom Baker's proposal (1938) that the forum lay to the rear of the colonnade, but faced east, with its basilica to the west. In spite of Richard Goodchild's suggestion in 1946 that Lincoln might represent one of the few British examples of a double-precinct forum, Richmond's view predominated until the excavations of 1978-9.

The various elements of the structures which constituted the civic centre are now discussed in turn, in order of their discovery, as a basis for an attempt to reconstruct the plan.

The Mint Wall

The 'Mint Wall' (**33**) has been a visible monument since its construction. It is an extremely rare survival in Britain of a Roman building wall, and lies in line with the most northerly of the columns found along Bailgate. It runs east-west for a distance of

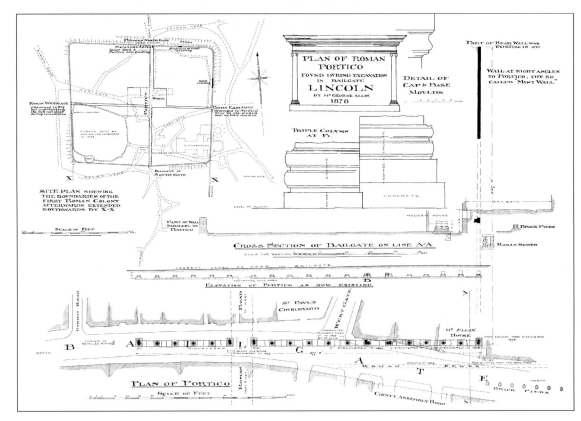

32 *Plan of remains of Bailgate colonnade and other nearby structures.* Produced by George Fox (*Archaeologia*, 1892). Society of Antiquaries of London

33 *The Mint Wall viewed from the south, looking west-north-west. Note the tile bonding courses, and their increased frequency at the eastern end*

*c.*23m, and stands all *c.*7m above the present ground-surface, which is a good 2m above its base. No windows are discernible. It is about 1m thick, being faced with of small blocks (referred to by French scholars as *petit appareil*) of limestone. At vertical intervals of *c.*1.5m, there are triple bonding-courses of *sesquipedales* tiles, each half the width of the wall (1.5 Roman feet square), a type of construction known as *opus vittatum mixtum* and common in Gaul from the late first century AD. The tile courses were a device to reinforce the weak structural point between facing and core, as well as being decorative. Immediately above each triple band are square holes for timber scaffolding (putlogs), a clue to the stages in which construction proceeded. Extra double courses of tile provided at the eastern end of the surviving section are likely to mean that there was a weak point in the form of a corner or arch adjacent. Analysis of the wall's mortar showed that it contained a high lime content, suggesting that it had been plastered.

The building of the North District School (immediately south of the wall) in 1852, revealed a 'beautiful pavement'. Grimm's depiction of the wall shows the stub of an adjoining wall apparently of tile running southwards from its west end, and other walls were noted *c.*16m and *c.*29m to the west of the colonnade, but the validity of their identification is uncertain. It did, however, prove possible to excavate small trenches both south and north of the Mint Wall in 1979 and 1980 respectively, following hard on the investigations on the forum east range (described below). In 1987-8 a detailed survey of the standing wall itself was carried out.

The work on the south side revealed an *opus signinum* floor similar to that being found in forum's east range further south, but at a higher level. The line of a robbed-out east-west wall *c*.13m south of the Mint Wall indicated either an aisle or the outside wall: the floor-level south of it, presumably that of a portico, was *c*.800mm lower than to the north (and incidentally at the same level as the portico in the east range). The floor itself was so worn that it had been repaired, with cobbles, possibly because it was on the line of a much-used entrance. Another east-west wall was found *c*.7m to the south – the same width as the internal portico in the east range.

Work in 1980 on the north side of the Mint Wall revealed an underlying structure, part of what had been a semi-circular pier facing northwards, probably built in the early second century. Finds included two ceramic antefixes (decorative ends to the ridge-tiles) with female heads, probably used as the gable-end of its roof. This structure had been demolished to make way for the building of which the Mint Wall was the northern boundary, in the late second or early third century.

The Bailgate colonnade

The second major element of the civic centre consists of the colonnade already mentioned which began to emerge in 1878; elements were still being revealed in 1897 (**32 & 35**). In 1879 the Roman sewer was found nearby, as well as a milestone lying between the two sets of double columns opposite the main east-west street, presumably an entrance. Its inscription gave the distance to *Segelocum* (Littleborough, on the River Trent) as 14 miles (*RIB* 2241). The rest of the colonnade, in all *c*.84m (275ft) long, was found in 1891 and 1897. Immediately to its south was a paved road, then a chamfered corner block, another significant discovery whose identification is problematic. The bronze foreleg of a horse, thought to be part of an imperial equestrian statue, may also have come from this area (**34**).

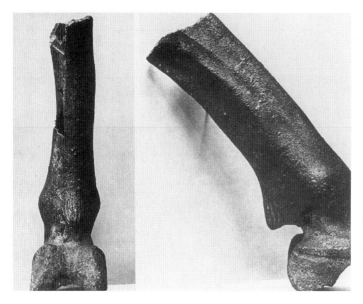

34 *Two views of the bronze foreleg of a horse, probably found in the Bailgate area, and possibly from a statue of the emperor on horseback.* Society of Antiquaries of London

1 *Mosaic found to the north of Exchequergate in approximately 1879*

2 *Tombstone of the veteran C. Iulius Galenus, formerly of the Sixth Legion found west of the walled area (RIB 252).*
British Museum

3 *Enamelled bronze pendant, probably from a harness, found in the nineteenth century.*
British Museum

4 *The Witham Shield, the best of a fine collection of Iron Age metalwork from the Witham Valley. Found east of Lincoln in 1826.* British Museum

5 *Replica of the tombstone of Titus Valerus Pudens of Legio II Adiutrix. Note the adze (ascia) in the bottom panel, a tool used for dressing stone.* P. Washbourn

6 *Artist's reconstruction of Late Iron Age huts close to the water.* City and County Museum

7 *Glass phials from the cremations, for anointing the body with oil*

8 *Painted wall-plaster from the Greetwell Villa*

9 *Mosaic found when the county prison inside the castle was extended in 1846*

10 *Dedication stone set up in AD 237 by M. Aurelius Lunaris, a priest of the Imperial cult in Lincoln and York*

11 *Relief sculpture of Cupid and Psyche from the Hungate house*

13 *Painted wall-plaster from a house on Silver Street later demolished to make way for the city fortifications*

14 *Plan of the remains of the Greetwell Villa*

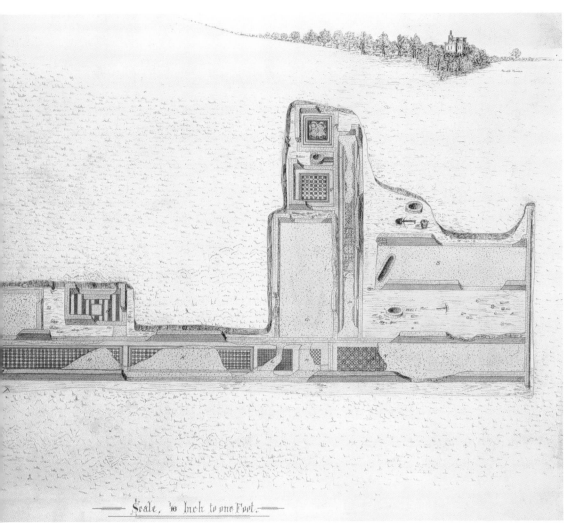

12 *The mosaic pavement from the eastern corridor of the Greetwell Villa*

Scale, ⅟₁₀ Inch to one Foot.

15 Legionary dagger-scabbard (possibly belonging to a centurion), with inlaid pattern in silver, from East Bight excavations

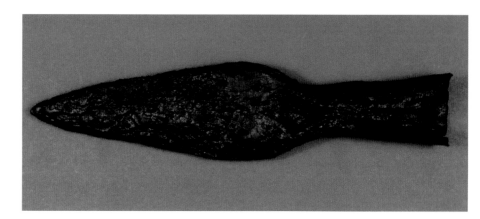

16 Spearhead from excavations at 181-3 High Street, on the site of the former Iron Age houses

17 Sherd with graffito mentioning 'salted olives'

18 *Fragment of painted wall plaster with floral designs found in the make-up for the rebuilt forum, and possibly derived from the early forum*

19 *Mosaic found in the cloisters of Lincoln Cathedral, 1792*

20 *Some samian tableware vessels found in the city, made in Gaul*

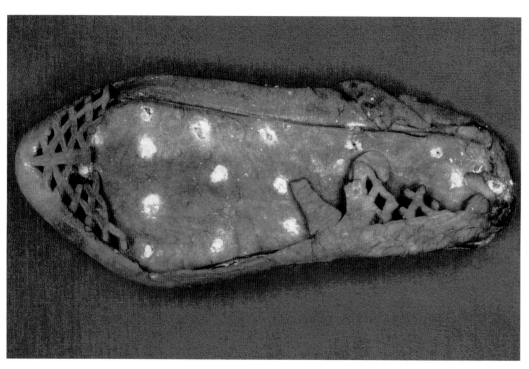

21 *One of the seventy or so Roman shoes from the Waterside North excavations*

22 *Gold ring from trader's house in the southern suburb*

23 *Gold earring from trader's house in the southern suburb*

24 *Bronze duck-brooch from trader's house in the eastern suburb*

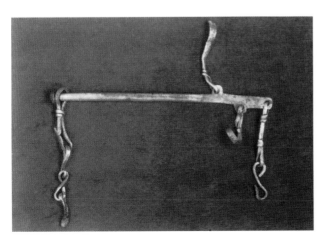

25 *Copper-alloy balance, from the Waterside North excavations*

26 *The charioteer sculpture; possibly from a youth organisation in the city*

27 *Sculpture of boy with pet hare*

28 *Sculptural relief thought to represent the guardian spirit of the city*

29 *Statuette of Mars from the Fossdyke canal.* British Museum

35 *Discovery of the colonnade, 1878*

Of the nineteen columns, some were double, and one even triple, interosculating (i.e. 'kissing', **35**). They were set *c*.4.8m apart centre to centre, with wider spacings of *c*.6m where there were double or triple columns, presumably to support (arched) entrances. One was on the line of the *decumanus* linking east and west gates, and another further north, perhaps at the junction between the basilica and the forum. At *c*.750-800mm in diameter, a height of *c*.7-9m can be estimated, but the spacing of the columns has more in common with those of the Leicester forum – at 6.5 times the column diameter – than the more normal 8 times of other known examples in Britain. In terms of its architectural ornament generally, however, it displays links with both southern Britain and the military zone. The column capitals are of the type thought to derive from one known in north-east Gaul. The columns themselves were not of local limestone, but coarse sandstone from the Pennines, which had special load-bearing qualities.

Excavations in the forum area

Other early discoveries were of a modest nature, and comprised only small details which at the time hardly improved our understanding. Finds of tessellated pavements were made to the south of the Mint Wall during the rebuilding of St Paul's church in the 1870s, and adjacent to the colonnade in 1897. In 1962-3, a small trench further south on Bailgate (to the rear of number 19, the Midland Bank) revealed the junction of a north-south wall, containing a gap for a doorway, with an east-west wall. There were some disturbed flagstone fragments at a lower level, and a later concrete floor and black-and-white mosaic pavement (considered by some to be of second-century date). These discoveries indicated two phases of substantial building whose function at the time could not be determined. A sequence of investigations beginning in 1976 and lasting until 1979, however, produced some major discoveries. They were subsequently supplemented by observations made during pipeline installations in 1982 and 1992-3, which have added a great deal. These are now described in turn.

In 1976, foundation trenches for a new house to the rear of number 2 West Bight, to the west of the Mint Wall, revealed a north-south stone wall, incorporating tile bonding-courses. This building had two phases of floor on its west side, the first of mortar, the second floor of slate flags. In 1978-9 larger-scale work was possible on the site of the former church of St Paul-in-the-Bail, extending for almost 50m to the west of Bailgate. It was here that the legionary *principia* was found. Overlying much of its site was a badly-preserved surface, originally pebbled but later paved, at least in part, and bounded to the east by a stone wall. The paved surface continued to the east of the wall – it was here very well-preserved (**36**), before it was later replaced by a double range of rooms, each leading out on to porticoes, one facing on to the paved courtyard to the west, and the other towards the Bailgate colonnade and the principal street to the east (**37**).

The above account is a simplification of the complex stratigraphy and various features excavated. There were other features which might belong to the earliest phases of the *colonia*, but their remains were fragmentary and difficult to interpret:

36 *Paving of the early forum-temple precinct, with base for possibly an equestrian statue. The wall on the left may only have been constructed for the later forum*

37 *Excavations of the east range of the forum, 1979. The level of the early paving is visible left; the floor level of the rebuilt forum lay a little above the offset on the well-head*

pits and patches of burning (both possibly associated with building work), several phases of surfacing, and a possible timber colonnade or hall. Timber basilicas have been found at Exeter – here as a temporary measure while the stone version was under construction – and possibly at Silchester.

The early forum-temple?

The first definite *colonia* structure was the well-preserved paved surface, with statue bases. From its condition, it may only have been in use for a short period, or was perhaps in a location which did not receive much wear. The north-south wall (**36**) may already have been in place in this early phase. If so, it was part of a major public structure containing a paved floor, or precinct, with statues, which fronted on to the main street to the east. The make-up for its successor contained debris which may have been derived from this early building – columns faced with fluted mouldings, and fine-quality wall-paintings (**colour plate 18**). The paving was identical to that found *c*.30m to the south in 1962-3. The semi-circular stone pier (noted above) found beneath the Mint Wall might have formed part of the same structure or an associated one. It is uncertain whether the Bailgate colonnade belonged to the same phase. Most probably, the remains represent some form of civic centre, possibly a forum with a temple whose significance is discussed further below.

The forum redesigned

A major redesign of the complex, which probably involved the construction of the Mint Wall, appears to have taken place at the end of the second century or in the first decades of the third. It involved a resurfacing of the courtyard, with a (robbed) stone gutter around its edge. If the north-south wall mentioned above had already existed, it was now reduced to a stylobate (plinth) for a colonnade overlooking the piazza to the west. To the east of the wall, the revised layout consisted of a double range of rooms entered via internal and external porticoes. These rooms, of various sizes and including some of semi-circular form, were constructed from the level of the early paving, although their floors were raised *c.*1m higher (**37** & **38**). Three rooms leading on to the western, internal portico 6m wide were identified, as well as two rooms to the east, and others to the north and south can be presumed (see plan). The external portico was even wider, at 7m. This rebuild provides a context for the Bailgate colonnade.

The well, now surmounted by four tile arches (**39**), was accessed principally via a small room to the west: the foundations for two successive water-butts were found here. The internal floors of the large eastern room leading on to the main street were usually of clay, with residues indicating industrial or commercial use: copper- and silver-working, and pottery, coins and vessel-glass all suggestive of a shop or refreshment area.

Several architectural fragments, including a moulded cornice, and imported marble from later deposits provide further details of the building, but the 'concrete' floors facing on to the internal courtyard were kept clean and produced little in the way of contemporary artefacts. The various rooms continued to be used at least into the late fourth century.

Synthesis

It is clear that a new precinct was being built in stone in the early second century and that underwent at least one major redesign by the early third century. The earlier of the two stone buildings was probably focused on a temple. It included an extensive paved area with statues, and a (probably separate) structure incorporating a pier to its north-west. Fora and temples occasionally display such piers in precinct walls: for

38 *Excavations of the east range of the forum, looking east, with the level of the* opus signinum *floor visible*

39 *The forum well-head, supported on tile arches*

instance, at Bavay in north-east France, in the basilica wall at Annecy, in the temple precinct of the forum at St Bertrand-de-Comminges in south-west France, and at the Forum Caesaris in Rome, remodelled in the early second century. There was considerable official investment in religious structures in the early stages of Romano-British cities, and this appears to have been particularly the case in the *coloniae*. The precinct at Colchester was rededicated to the Emperor Claudius after his death in AD 54, and further developed from the end of the first century, as the two new *coloniae* were being established. The Westgate colonnade at Gloucester is now considered to have belonged to a huge temple precinct larger than its forum-basilica. It seems therefore quite possible that there was a similar large precinct at Lincoln, possibly confined to a temple-forum.

It was not unusual for public monuments to be modified or thoroughly redesigned, and sometimes enlarged, as at London and at Conimbriga in Portugal. There were several phases at other well-known complexes at Velleia and Aquileia in Italy. The excavations have now set the various elements of the replanned forum at Lincoln into place. The Mint Wall can thus be identified as the north wall of a civic basilica *c*.13m wide, with a portico to the south, lying to the north of the forum courtyard and east range beneath St Paul-in-the-Bail. The north-south extent of the civic centre might thus be co-terminous with the colonnade. The symmetry of the whole complex was corroborated by the remains subsequently recorded in a number of service-trenches (**40**). The building seen in 1976 at West Bight was therefore identified as the next block west of the forum. Trenches along Westgate also indicated another major public building to the west.

But was it a double-precinct forum, consisting of basilica, forum, and temple precinct? This idea was particularly supported by the affinity between the layout of the complex at Lincoln and the examples at Paris and at Augst, near Basle in Switzerland. This idea was reinforced by the finding of fragments of an inscription in Purbeck marble, re-used in the foundations of one of the churches, referring to the rebuilding

40 *Reconstruction drawing of the rebuilt forum, looking south. Note temple precinct (conjectural) beyond; the temple may have faced eastwards, on to the main street, rather than back towards the forum*

of a temple by a priest of the imperial cult. If the return wall found in 1962-3 defined the southern limit, however, there would be insufficient room for a temple in the southern part of the precinct, facing the basilica. An alternative location for a small temple might lie within the west or south range, as suggested at Velleia in Italy.

A separate temple precinct is another possibility. There was, for example, a wall separating the main courtyard from the temple precinct at Nyon, in Switzerland, and a clear division at Virunum on the Danube. That at St Bertrand-de-Comminges faced away from the forum on to the main street. It is therefore possible that a temple precinct may have existed to the south. The solid corner block to the south of the colonnade may only represent a *spina* before the colonnade continued: the Bailgate colonnade falls well short of the normal length of the double precinct forum. The chamfered corner is, however, best interpreted as that of a podium for a temple facing east on to the main street.

The basilica appears to have had a simple plan (resembling that at Djemila/Cuicul in North Africa). It was at least 9m high. The hint of an *exedra* (recess), whether rectangular or semi-circular, in the centre of the north wall could be interpreted in several possible ways: the site of a small temple, offices, the *curia* (council room) as found in the second phase at Augst, or merely an architectural feature perhaps housing a statue. The council room might alternatively have been located at one end of the basilica, or in the south range, facing it (as suggested for Verulamium) or even along another side. The floor with quarter-round moulding found adjacent to the north-south wall in the basilica may represent the lower floor of a heated room – perhaps a tribunal (platform) at a higher level.

In summary, while the later forum at Lincoln may or may not have contained a temple, in its long colonnaded frontage, with double side entrances into the forum, and in its wide double ranges, it stands clearly apart from the so-called 'principia-type' forum found at most *civitas* capitals in Britain. As much of the architectural inspiration for Roman Britain came from north-east Gaul, one might assume influences from sites such as Bavay, which had a double-precinct forum. Lincoln's architectural decoration shared links with both the south-east of Britain and the military and civilian centres of the north Midlands, and at times with sites further north like York and Catterick. In other ways it was outside the Romano-British mainstream. We can at least be sure that its civic centre, the tallest and largest building at both the centre and the highpoint of the city, succeeded in impressing visitors.

The public baths

Communal bathing was an essential ingredient of the Roman urban lifestyle, with perceived social and health benefits. The bathing establishments built to serve cities or whole legions were huge complexes, requiring much in the way of fuel and water to meet popular demand. Those at Lincoln, which were identified in 1957 by Dennis Petch, were situated in the north-east sector of the city, close to the northern defences and to the water tank adjacent to the city wall nearby. It is possible that the exercise hall did front on to the main street, but the excavations suggested that the complex had faced south, being entered via a colonnaded façade leading eastwards from the main street. Although these investigations were on a large scale and took many months, the fact that the work was undertaken in a series of small trenches with volunteers working intermittently means that the various discrete remains are difficult to piece together (**41**). The brief summary of the discoveries presented here is based on a draft report prepared by Mr Petch, but it is hoped that resources will be found to complete the analysis of the structures and of the rich collection of artefacts found. Of the many rooms uncovered, some were provided with deep hypocausts for under-floor heating, as well as floors of stone flags and tessellated pavements (**42**). One wall, about 2.5m thick, was presumably close to the furnace. There was also a douche, with a gutter. The fragmentary elements of the layout revealed unfortunately do not fit obviously into any of the various blueprints for plan type, either military or civilian (and there was some cross-fertilisation between the two).

The Lincoln baths covered an area of at least 60 x 45m, and were twice extended to the west, sealing an existing north-south street in the process (**25**). These extensions appear to date to the mid- to late second century. The original *colonia* baths can probably be assigned to the first half of the second century, and may even have incorporated legionary elements. This would not be an unusual location for legionary baths, but parts of the site had previously been occupied by legionary timber structures. Like those of the later forum, and others noted below, some of the walls incorporated brick courses. Among the remains of building materials from the site (and from several others in the city) was a number of stamped tiles, the stamps recording the workshop and batch number. These tiles are considered to belong to the Hadrianic period (AD 117-38). The site also produced important collections of

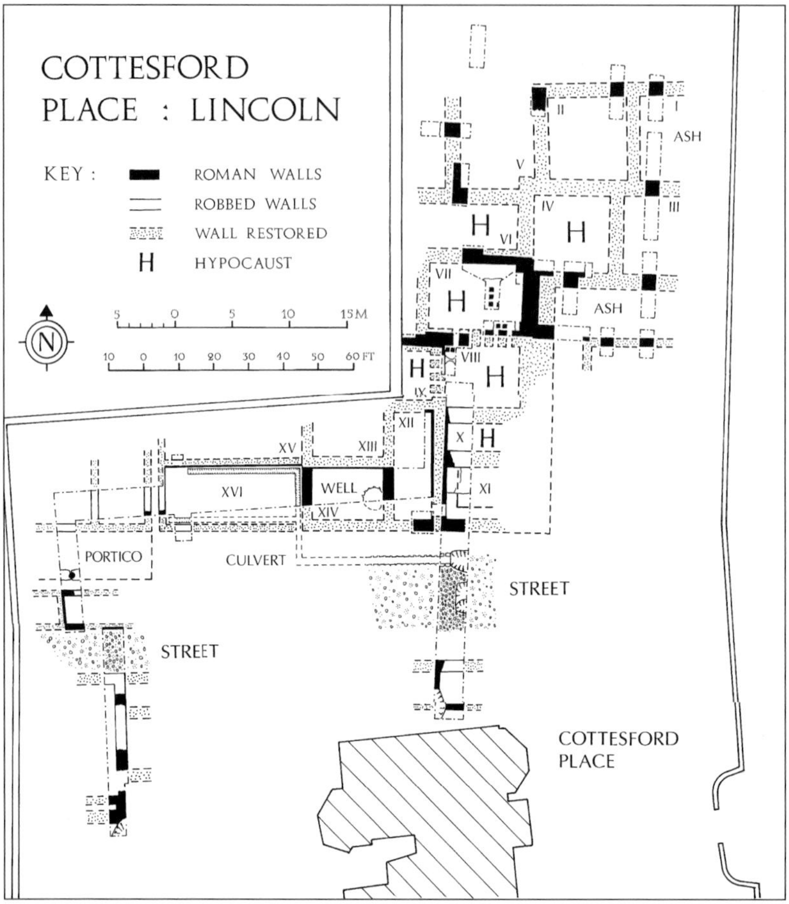
COTTESFORD PLACE : LINCOLN
KEY :
ROMAN WALLS
ROBBED WALLS
WALL RESTORED
H
HYPOCAUST
N
5 0 5 10 15M
10 0 10 20 30 40 50 60 FT
ASH
ASH
STREET
STREET
PORTICO
CULVERT
WELL
COTTESFORD PLACE

41 *Plan of the excavations at Cottesford Place, 1957, which revealed the public bath sand shops to the south.* D.F. Petch

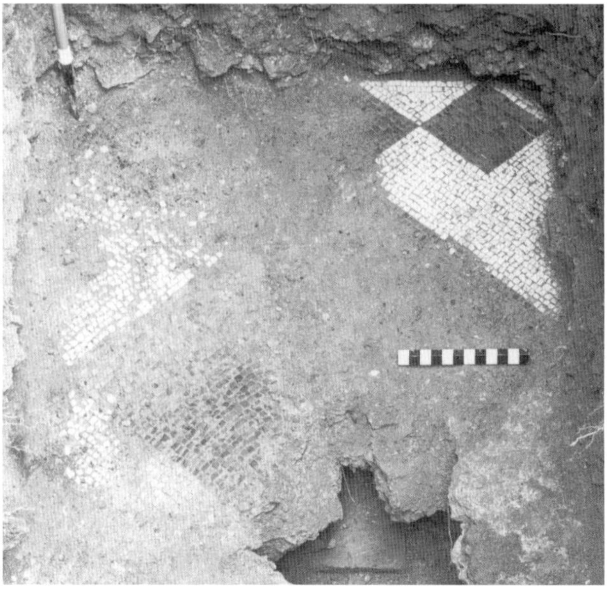

42 *Floor of public baths with black and white tessellated pavement*

samian ware (fine pottery made in Gaul) and vessel glass of the late first to early second century, marble inlays from the Mediterranean, and a shale object thought to be part of a chair leg.

Lost spectacles?

The amphitheatre, the main focus of public entertainments, has not yet come to light, but it would presumably have represented a consolidation of any military predecessor (chapter 4), and have stood outside one of the gates on the level ground to the west, east or north. A location to the west, outside the fortress' *porta decumana* (the rear gate), was, while not universal, most common, and certainly the area to the north of the street running out westwards has not produced significant evidence for other structures. If, like most in Roman Britain, it was essentially an earth and timber structure, later levelling might have removed just about any trace of its former existence: even in London, the arena was only located by chance in 1988. Certainly, the fact that at the west end of the street of Westgate, Roman military levels occur immediately beneath the ground-surface shows that earth-moving operations were taking place at some stage, perhaps to fill the Castle ditch. Whatever their date, these works also levelled the former Roman rampart. Similar operations could have obliterated the banks of the amphitheatre. What makes this idea particularly worth pursuing is the fact that there may have been an Anglo-Saxon meeting place in the area to the north-west of the west gate: an arena was where the Roman population too had gathered. The greatest concentration of pottery of the mid-Saxon period (eighth to ninth century) in Lincoln came from the grounds of The Lawn nearby: the presence of an amphitheatre may explain why. Some other amphitheatres in Britain were re-used for different purposes in the post-Roman period, and it is possible that the example at Lincoln was considered a suitable venue, as a major landmark. This is still speculation, of course, but an idea worth following up by future fieldwork.

It is of course possible that the legionary *ludus* (training arena) was demolished and not converted to a civilian arena, or even that none was ever provided. Whether the *colonia* had an amphitheatre or not, it would expect to number a theatre among its amenities, perhaps linked to a temple. There are several candidates, represented by slight traces of monumental structures along the two principal streets of the city. Apart from the substantial structure (probably a temple) immediately to the south of the known later forum, there was another across the main north-south street: a wall containing tile courses in its fabric appeared north of Eastgate in 1848. Further to the south, fragments of a fluted column, the base of an engaged column, and walls noted at various times suggested part of a monumental entrance, or archway.

A row of eight brick piers, with semi-circular fronts, came to light at the same time as the Bailgate colonnade, but across the street and extending northwards from the northern limit of the colonnade. Bricks were used in this way to represent engaged columns. Remains of a colonnade found further east, at Atton Place to the north of the west front of the cathedral, may indicate either another monumental frontage or surround of a building to the south of the main east-west street.

Several substantial north-south walls were noted in pipe-laying operations in 1992 to the west of the forum. They were as much as 2m thick, and incorporated tile courses. These would be best interpreted as a building facing southwards on to the main east-west street, the *decumanus*. A mortar floor was noted between two of the walls, but too little of their plan was revealed to identify the building's function. Further west along Westgate, two parallel north-south walls *c*.5m apart were noted in advance of and during construction work in 1989; painted wall-plaster was associated with it which suggests that these remains are more likely to be a house, and it is to the rest of the evidence for residential accommodation that we now turn.

Commerce and housing

To the south of the street on to which the baths faced, there were other structures, probably commercial in nature. There are likely to have been a large number of similar establishments in the upper city, apart from those already noted in the east frontage of the forum, but not such a great concentration as outside the walls. Traders' houses, buildings devoted principally to commerce with accommodation attached, have been identified just beyond the gates. They took the form usually found in Britain, of long narrow structures, gable-end on to the street.

We actually have little evidence for the houses of the upper city. No modern excavations have been possible to compare with the results from the other *coloniae*, where some of the earliest houses consisted of modified barrack-blocks. The barracks at Colchester were standing for no more than five years before the legion left, and it made sense to re-use them. The sequence at Gloucester is not so clear, but it is possible that there was a rebuilding shortly before the army left. During the transitional period at Lincoln, the military buildings revealed to date were at least in part dismantled.

In the earliest years of the *colonia*, accommodation for the new administrative and religious centres was the priority. The earliest houses at Lincoln, of which we have found only small fragments, were provided with walls of timber, in some cases on stone sills. In the cities of Roman Britain generally, whether colonies or not, few large town houses are known before the mid-second century. By the third and fourth centuries they were attracting greater investment, and were grander, with substantial stone walls and more lavish decoration. They might still include an area for business and their frontages could be used, even let out, for commercial purposes. Some of them are indicated by the mosaic pavements found principally during building operations in the eighteenth and nineteenth centuries, often in connection with hypocausts. They include examples from within the area of the castle (**colour plate 9**), the cathedral and its precincts (**colour plate 19**), at the top of Steep Hill, at the north end of Bailgate, and near to and beneath the 1911 water tower further west. The artistic quality of the mosaics is not generally considered to be in the first rank of those from Britain, a view partly stemming from the fragmentary nature of the evidence, and the survival of designs largely limited to geometric patterns. Some of the buildings containing mosaics were also graced with wall paintings, part of the decorative ensemble.

7 Planned growth: the lower walled city

In the legionary period, most of the structures to the south of the fortress had lined the road leading from the south gate to the river crossing. By the mid-second century, the hillside below the upper city (sometimes known as the 'Enlarged Colonia') was being formally planned with new streets, and the land was gradually being occupied. Good evidence of this process was found at The Park, on the line of the later western defences and c.200m to the west of Ermine Street. Here, timber buildings set at right angles to the street must have related to an existing street grid. Development soon spread laterally across the hillside so far to the east and west that, when the lower city was in due course fortified, buildings including those at The Park (near to the 'lower west gate') and others on the east side had to be demolished to make way. The line of the new defences logically followed a direct extension southwards of the uphill circuit to the line of the then riverfront.

The evidence for land use which has accumulated over more than two centuries suggests that the Ermine Street frontage, at least on the lower, gentler slope, was occupied by several public monuments. There may also have been houses, but on the whole, residential developments were confined to the land to the east and west, as well as to that higher up the slope (25). By the third century, the lower city could boast several signs of Roman urban sophistication, not least in the houses, which were growing in scale. The fourth-century townscape was dominated by these large residences for the elite. Further strengthening of the fortifications during the same period created a considerable barrier, which like the houses must have absorbed substantial resources. Hints from a number of sites indicate survival of urban life into the early fifth century, but a much reduced population with little economic activity, and no definite occupation beyond this date (chapter 12).

Development of the very steep slope (approximately 1 in 6) in the higher part of the clay hillside marked by springs, and the risk of subsidence, involved considerable risks and practical difficulties. The regular nuisance of excess water was to some extent counteracted by constructing culverts and drains. Some ran parallel to the north-south streets; near to the eastern defences, there was also a timber supply pipe on the opposite side of the street, but still the amount of silt on the road-surfaces suggests that they would have been awash during periods of heavy rain. A substantial stone drain at the house (also provided with wooden water pipes) in Hungate became blocked (43). There may even have been pools and flowing streams: water-logged deposits found north of Saltergate, perhaps in a garden, and the watercourse

43 *Drain in the garden of a house at Hungate, later blocked*

flowing into the river at Waterside North *c.*100m to its south, might best be interpreted in this way. Other streams or inlets may have existed outside the line of the defences (see below). Further down the hill, the sandy terrace – flatter, drier and better-draining – was not so beset with these problems.

Origins and growth

Several sites have produced first-century artefacts associated with the military occupation, not all close to Ermine Street: for instance, a first-century Rhodian *amphora* turned up in the early levels at Spring Hill. It is fairly certain that in the legionary period the hillside was under the army's control, and it is likely that it was subsequently included within the original boundary (*pomerium*) of the *colonia*. The area may then have been defined physically in some way prior to the erection of the fortifications, its status rationalised by the imposition of a street grid and the construction of defences. An alternative view would see the immigrants and local traders formerly in the legionary *canabae* constituting the majority of the original settlers on the hillside, which would have been given the status of a *vicus*, with full *colonia* status only coming later. It may have had to wait until the enfranchisement of all freeborn citizens of the Empire in 213 by the Emperor Caracalla, an edict known as the *Constitutio Antoninana*. By this time fortifications were at least under construction and the residences of local aristocrats were dominating the area. Whatever its legal status, it is generally accepted that the lower city was part of the new town from the start.

Some of the earliest evidence for its occupation has emerged at the subsequent east and west limits of the walled city (**22**): this may merely reflect accidents of survival and investigation, but these early clusters could also indicate that inlets of the river existed to the west and east of the later walls. Buildings resembling grain stores have been found at both sites, buried beneath the later ramparts. Other early structures, all presumably domestic, appear to be aligned on to a street grid set by the alignment of Ermine Street. Evidence from nine different excavations confirm the impression of a planned layout by the middle of the second century. Most of the earliest structures were houses of timber, of a modest scale but internally well-appointed, but others might have been for commercial use.

Topographical development: terraces and streets

The parallel walls observed by Michael Drury in 1888 near to the top of Steep Hill, the lower one being 4.5m thick, were considered by Richmond to represent part of a major terracing across a good part of the hill, resembling that at Tarragona in Spain. It could have created an artificial platform *c.*45m wide. An alternative possibility is that the terrace could have represented part of the theatre structure, with the *cavea* (auditorium) facing southwards – a good use of the slope, but also requiring major engineering to support the south side. Normally a theatre was located within the walls, but the south-facing slope had its attractions. Terracing elsewhere on the slope has been noted within and between properties, but few excavations have taken place on the steepest part of the slope, while later post-Roman attempts to stabilise structures may have cut into and removed much of the Roman evidence. The recent investigations at the upper south gate indicate that its ground level was only just below the present, with bedrock visible in the later cellar. Being used as an archway for so many centuries, the level was maintained.

Some earlier ideas about the street pattern, based on the idea that the Roman grid was largely re-used in the medieval period, have now been shown to be erroneous. Excavations have demonstrated that the town had to be re-planned from the late ninth century, and earlier ideas that the Roman street pattern can still be discerned have had to be jettisoned. Yet there has been substantial progress in locating streets of the Roman lower city. The major north-south route itself is of great interest: the line of Ermine Street itself appears to continue in a straight line up the steepest part of the hill. In 1984 its course was revealed between its medieval successors, Michaelgate and Steep Hill, in the form of monumental steps, interspersed with ramps (**44**). This is a feature without parallel in Roman Britain, but one known in the more hilly towns of the Mediterranean. The approach thereby created to the upper city, enhanced by the gate at the top, betrays the wish of the community to impress. Presumably it was constructed in the second century, when such ambitious public schemes were most common. It could not accommodate heavy wheeled vehicles, which had to follow an alternative line. The existence of diagonal routes was established in 1987 when a street with surfaces showing evidence of wheel ruts was noted at the bottom of Steep Hill, near to the point where the gradient becomes steep (**25**). The continuation of the route to the east of Steep Hill is possibly that followed by Well Lane and Danesgate, providing a winding but easier incline at about half the gradient of the direct route: a good parallel can be found at Cassino in Italy. This discovery helped to clarify why the Roman house found on Steep Hill adjacent was set at an oblique angle – it respected the alignment of the diagonal street.

Traces of the parallel north-south street to the west of Ermine Street were indicated on Spring Hill, the form of a rough surface, and, higher up, two house walls *c*.6m apart. Another north-south street known, and in place from the early second century, lay inside the eastern defences (which it pre-dated), with a pavement or portico to its east. There were possibly two more between this street and Ermine Street. One ran northwards from the small postern gate in the south wall on Saltergate, immediately west of Bank Street. The other may be indicated by a gap between structures found during foundation works in 1956 beneath the Co-op building in Silver Street.

There is some uncertainty about the principal east-west route across the hillside – it now appears that the grids either side of Ermine Street were planned separately, or at least offset, as at Cirencester (**25**). With the route between the east and west gates still evading detection, the exact positions of the gates themselves are also subject to confirmation, although the west gate almost certainly lay on the line of West Parade. Certainly there was a gate by the tenth century where the street now called Clasketgate passed through the east wall. The Roman street was not found in excavations immediately north or south of Grantham Street, and a line further south making for the gate would be more likely, but it might also have lain several metres to the north. An alternative possibility is that the street's alignment was oblique to that of the main grid, and was represented by that of a stone foundation at Flaxengate running from north-north-west to south-south-east and possibly linking the gate directly to Ermine Street or forming part of a winding route for vehicles. There may have been several other streets taking similarly easier gradients; if there had been a major terrace higher up, it may have dictated or at least constrained the street layout.

44 *Monumental steps on the line of Ermine Street, on the steep part of the hill, found 1984*

Another east-west street must have lain on the line of the inserted gateway at The Park, on the western defences. This gate here lies only *c.*100m to the south of West Parade, probably the site of an existing gateway. Burials are known from the extra-mural area nearby, both along the line of West Parade and further to the south and south-west. The internal buildings found north of West Parade must have fronted on to a nearby north-south street not far from the present line of Beaumont Fee. There was also a street outside the walls next to the riverside, on the north side of what later became Saltergate.

In summary, the lower city was provided with a street grid, but did not have such a rigorous system as that in the upper city, partly for historical reasons, and partly because of the difficult topography of the steeper slope. The line of Ermine Street was the focus. Where examined, all of the streets continued in use to the late Roman period, and some to the end of Roman occupation.

Fortifications

Parts of the city wall were still prominent into the eighteenth century, although much of the facing had been removed, largely to disappear from view over the next two centuries. Although the first systematic investigation of the sequence did not take place until 1948, major excavations in the early 1970s have resulted in the structural sequence being now well-documented, but its dating is imprecise since it relies largely on the dates of material in or under the rampart bank which could have been decades old when it found its way there. It is in any case certain that construction began later than the layout of the street system, and involved the demolition of existing buildings on the line of the circuit, which essentially forms a southwards extension of the line of the upper city walls, but parallel to the slightly different alignment of Ermine Street.

There were apparent discrepancies between the west and east sides. An earth rampart *c.*7.5m wide and a contemporary wall *c.*1.2m thick and c.4m high were built on the west side at a date no earlier than the late second century (**45**). At Silver Street on the east, however, there was a line of substantial posts on the crest of the rampart, presumably for a fence or boxed structure. This may have been a temporary solution while construction of the stone wall – a slower process – was progressing around the circuit. Dating evidence from here suggested a date well into the third century for the construction of this feature, but evidence from an excavation only a little to the south in 1994 favours a date in the late second century, as on the west. If the later dating is correct, it may mean that such a huge circuit (*c.*2km in length) took decades to build, or that the dating material from the other sites was largely residual and misleading.

A construction date in the early third century is associated by some scholars with Caracalla's act of universal citizenship, but this may only have raised the status of the lower city if it were not already regarded as formally part of the *colonia*. It may simply have followed a request to the Emperor for permission to enclose the hillside.

79

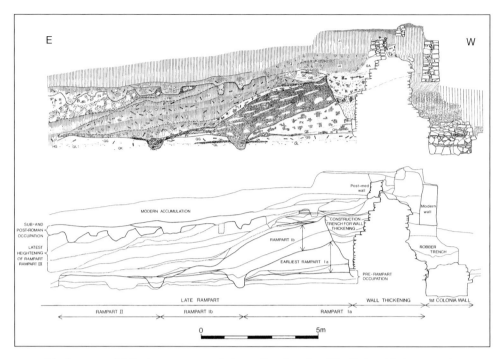

45 *Sequence of defensive ramparts and city wall as found at The Park, with interpretation*

Alternatively, it could have formed part of a provincial policy of enclosure being applied to all major Romano-British towns in this period, and perhaps reflected the growing awareness and importance of this part of the city. The development of the suburb to the south of the river may have allowed many of the traders to relocate, and thereby create more space for expansion of the elite residences within the lower city.

The first fortifications were surrounded by at least one ditch, later re-cut, and internal towers were added at intervals of *c*.40 or *c*.50m during the third century. The rampart was also extended, using dumps containing large amounts of rubbish, notably pottery, bone and jet artefacts (**83**), as well as animal bone. The identification of the east and west gates has already been mentioned. With regard to the south gate, an important structure that greeted all visitors from the south, a gate here documented in 1147 may have been a surviving Roman gate, or based on it. It is also conceivable that a monumental arch had stood here previously. There may have been several smaller postern gates, especially towards the riverfront: one was found *c*.100m east of the main south gate, but may have been a later insertion (**25** & **46**).

Another new gate was introduced into the existing circuit *c*.100m south of the west gate, on the site of an interval tower, in the mid- to late fourth century. Why it was needed is unclear. It was of a conservative plan type, and incorporated re-used blocks of monumental scale, from a funerary monument or a classical temple. Such re-use is fairly unusual in Britain, but many architectural fragments and tombstones have come to light in the rebuilt lower city wall, with especial concentrations by the south-west corner and on the east side. The wall adjacent to the postern gate at

Saltergate contained elements of a large dedicatory inscription from what must have been a structure of some importance, whose meaning unfortunately cannot be deciphered (**46**). At The Park, much of the rampart removed to create the new entrance was re-deposited on the adjacent rampart, increasing its width here to at least 16m; and more large groups of pottery, glass, and other artefacts were found in the dumps, as well as butchers' waste. As in the upper city, the city wall was thickened to a gauge of *c*.3m and heightened to *c*.7-8m. A wide 'saucer-shaped' ditch *c*.25m wide is probably contemporary; its cutting may have encroached on to the cemetery where some of the tombstones once stood.

Public monuments

As the lower city developed, it acquired a range of public structures along its main thoroughfare. Although those definitely identified are at present confined to the flatter, lower part of the Ermine Street frontage, this distribution may simply reflect that of excavation sites as much as the problems of the slope. The southern part of the frontage contained baths, a temple or shrine, and a fountain. The most northerly discovery of structures of similar character was found on the north side of Grantham Street, where Michael Drury recorded some moulded stones. About 60m east of here, along Grantham Street, the north-eastern part of what appeared to be a late Roman basilican building was revealed in 1975-6. Associated building materials, including a 'Tuscan' column-capital, mosaic *tesserae*, imported marble inlays, and window glass give some idea of its quality; several late Roman conical beakers echo this impression. Its apparent scale and layout suggested that it might be a church, or audience hall, whose construction could have followed from the city's elevation to capital status (chapter 11). Subsequent investigations on sites to its west and south have not borne out that hypothesis: the contemporary deposits had apparently been destroyed. As long as its plan remains unresolved so does its function, and residential use is not out of the question.

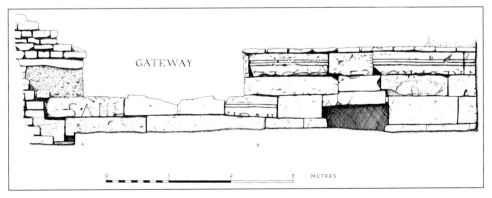

GATEWAY

0   1   2   3   METRES

46 *Elevation of the masonry of the postern-gate and adjacent city wall at Saltergate in the southern defences. The traces of huge letters of what must have formed an inscription of a dedication for a huge monumental building are visible, but not enough survives for it to be deciphered. N.M. Reynolds*

A little to the south, during construction works at 274-7 High Street in 1997, remains of what appeared to be a fluted column were pulled from a service trench on the edge of High Street. In the King's Arms Yard adjacent to the Theatre Royal, further south, part of a substantial baths building appeared in 1782, in the form of a heated room *c.*6m square. Nearby, under the corner of Clasketgate and High Street, the construction of a cellar for the original Boots store in 1924-5 uncovered a north-south wall *c.*4.5m long incorporating two flue arches (**3**). The next Roman find to the south lay beneath number 287 (now Ruddock's bookshop), and took the form of column bases, plinth or architrave stones and other architectural fragments, plus a significant inscription referring to the ward (*vicus*) of the guild of Mercury (*RIB* 270). The city was formally divided into such districts, identified by the various classical gods, and this was presumably the location of the shrine.

Just a little further down was an octagonal public fountain, discovered in 1830 and finally investigated in 1953. It was built of massive limestone blocks, with a lining (like the water tank in the upper city) of waterproof cement (*opus signinum*) (**47** & **48**); a tile surround rendered in red-painted plaster was a secondary feature, possibly added in order to seal the leaks from the main structure. It measured *c.*6m across, and a little over 1m in height. The existence of a channel for the outlet pipe confirmed its function. How it was supplied is less clear. It may have been fed by an aqueduct from above the hill or from the hillside: a pipeline was found at Greestone Stairs, east of the walled city, in 1857 which closely resembled the main aqueduct. The fountain probably stood in its own open court, on the edge of the street, and resembled other examples at Metz, in north-east Gaul, and the *colonia* at Timgad in Algeria. Immediately inside the south gate, column bases have been recorded on both sides of the street. The combination of all these classical structures provides clear evidence of the developing architectural sophistication of the lower city, and this was echoed by the investments made in private housing.

47 *The octagonal public fountain excavated in 1953*

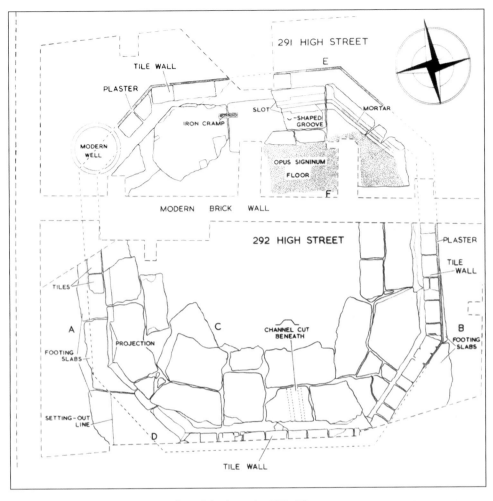

48 *Plan of the fountain.* F.H. Thompson

Housing

The chronological pattern of housing development in the Lower City, from the early second-century timber structures to increasingly large stone-built types, is not inconsistent with the general Romano-British picture of increasing scale from the mid-Roman period, but it would also be true to say that the earlier deposits have not been examined at several sites. The major rescue excavations of the 1970s and 1980s substantially increased our knowledge of residential development in the lower city, although the very scale of the larger late Roman houses meant that complete plans could not be recovered. The outstanding impression is of the size and quality of the later houses. This was a characteristic of other cities, so that the extent to which it resulted from the elevation to capital status in the fourth century, and from the spending power of government officials, is uncertain (chapter 11).

Remains of housing cover much of the hillside. Earlier discoveries included those east of Bank Street (found in 1936) – a heated room with red-painted walls, which adjoined other structures, in the form of several stone walls noted beneath the Co-op building in 1956. A hypocausted room was observed on Grantham Street a little to the west of Danesgate in 1836, and to its north-west was a house on the east side of Flaxengate (now a car park, but soon to be a new museum!), with marble inlayed surfaces, investigated in 1945-6.

The sequence of timber and stone structures found at The Park in 1970-2, all eventually buried beneath the later rampart, included some residential in nature, and others more suggestive of store buildings. These lay to the south of the street which led to the later gate, and to its north were more substantial walls. At a distance *c.*200m to the north, in what may have been a backwater well away from important routeways, the excavated remains suggest commercial or industrial activity allied with residential. On the other side of the city, close to the eastern defences, excavations between Silver Street and Broadgate in 1973 uncovered structures either side of a north-south street. Again, the earlier buildings were subsequently obliterated by the rampart, which here contained fragments of painted wall-plaster (**colour plate 13**): this was a relatively early house to be so well-decorated – did its presence delay the work on the fortifications at this point?

Among the later houses, there is much of interest to us. That found north of Spring Hill was first discovered when a mosaic pavement was saved by the then mayor from the destructive actions of a labourer's pick. Excavations in 1983-4 uncovered twelve rooms, including one with a hypocaust (**49**). Development of land to the north has provided indications of more houses either side of a north-south lane higher up the slope. A house revealed in 1973-4 to the south of the west end of Silver Street was provided with a channelled hypocaust, and window glass of the late Roman blown type was found in its demolition deposits. It covered an area at least 30m square inside the southern defences, not including a possible garden with a pond

49 *Hypocaust system of a house found on Spring Hill in 1983; it had mosaic floors and at least twelve rooms*

50 *Lower part of the wall of a house on Hungate, showing where wooden water pipes had run: the iron collars survived*

to the west. Other gardens, or at least open areas, are suggested at several sites. At a site between Hungate and High Street, a private water supply had been provided by wooden pipes whose iron collars survived (**50**). Here, in an open area (a garden?) was the stone drain which had become blocked (**43**). The plastered frame for a double door survived at ground level. This site also produced a second- or third-century relief sculpture (**colour plate 11**), box-tile, painted wall-plaster and the largest collection of window glass from any site in the lower city (only the public baths produced more). It continued in use into the late fourth century, as did at least one structure south of Grantham Street with late additions.

The late houses of the lower city confirm the impression provided by its public monuments that the hillside changed and developed considerably in the third century. They are assumed to be associated with citizens of power and influence who played significant political roles locally, the people who also might have sponsored some of the public works. Later, some may perhaps have belonged to the provincial government officials.

Social and economic life

The range of artefacts found in the lower city indicates the increasing evidence for both wealth and symbols of its display. The relief sculpture from the house at Hungate represents the mythical story of Cupid and Psyche (a local version of that described in Apuleius' *Golden Ass*). The inscription referring to the worshippers of Mercury has been mentioned above. A similar stone of the guild of Apollo (*RIB* 271) came from the rebuilt city wall. Late Roman finds such as a buckle and a brooch of 'Free German' origin may indicate nothing more than the fashion of the day, rather than the presence of Germanic mercenaries, but add to the picture of changing tastes.

The late wall also incorporated a large number of other inscribed and sculpted stones, some of them no doubt obtained from adjacent cemeteries. They included the tombstone of nonagenarian Claudia Crysis (*RIB* 263) and that of Volusia Faustina (*RIB* 250) (**24**), wife of the decurion Aurelius Senecio, plus altars to Mars (*RIB* 248) and that to the 'Goddesses, Fates, and Deities of the Emperor' still accessible in St

Swithin's Church. The same site produced the tombstone of the youth holding a hare (**colour plate 27**), while deities associated with *cornucopiae* (horns of plenty) were found at Newland and just outside the city wall on Monks Road, interpreted as the personification (*tyche*) of the city, and generally regarded as one of the finest pieces from Lincoln (**colour plate 28**). While their place in the cemeteries is discussed below, the culture they express, and the quality of some of the finest pieces, confirm the presence of a literate Latin-speaking elite in Britain.

This evidence for visible cultural expressions can be set against that of the pottery and other artefacts. The lower city had the highest proportion of table to kitchen wares for the city. There are fewer drinking vessels than the southern suburb, but the general profile is closer to the suburbs than to the Upper City. Superficially, the reasons for this may of course be due to the nature and chronology of the sites investigated – for instance, there has been little modern excavation of houses in the Upper City, and most of the deposits excavated in the Lower City have been of a comparatively late date. However, it is interesting to compare the ceramic assemblage with the glass: the later Roman vessel glass from the Lower City forms a large collection, and includes some high-quality items. Many vessels were used for liquid consumption and for the display and serving of food – as might be expected from the aristocratic residences in an era of social competition.

Before the late Roman period, we have little evidence from the Lower City for industrial activity. This is likely to be a true impression, as, until the late fourth century, industry seems for the most part to have been confined to extra-mural areas. The adjacent site to the east of the walled area contained a furnace for iron smelting (and perhaps also smithing), in the grounds of a residence which later had a baths suite added, and copper alloy was worked nearby. Moulds for producing counterfeit silver coins, a common phenomenon at a time of shortage in the late second and early third centuries, were found at two sites, one just outside the east gate. In the later period, organised butchery was being practised on a large scale; dumps of waste were found at Flaxengate, on the rampart at The Park, and particularly in the fourth century at the Waterside sites.

In the later fourth century, there was also iron-working at Hungate, possible gold- and silver-working at Flaxengate and Saltergate, and a trader's oven north of West Parade. Some of the commercial activity could well have been confined to the last decades of the Roman period, when the nature of the town was changing rapidly and there may have been a shift to a more self-sufficient economic basis. Were these the last throes of the Roman system, or was it merely suburban traders seeking security by moving inside the walls as others left? These questions are discussed in context in chapters 11 and 12.

8 Expansion beyond the walls

Occupation of the area outside what became the walled town began early in the life of the settlement. The river was essential for fishing and communication, land on its banks for settlement and warehousing, and the areas used for burial in the legionary period lay further south in the valley. Structures on the hillside below the fortress and outside the other gates probably housed the *canabae*.

Following the foundation of the *colonia*, the land outside the former gates of the fortress was more extensively developed from the second century: one of the achievements of the last quarter-century of research has been to demonstrate the extensive growth of these suburbs. Previously, knowledge of extra-mural occupation was principally confined to the cemeteries, and finds such as the mosaic pavements on Monson Street were thought to indicate a villa at the edge of the settlement: it is now clear that it formed either a continuation of the cemetery or part of the suburban sprawl. To the south, ribbon development extended for at least 1km beyond the walls (**25**). There was similar development outside the other gates, but nowhere so extensive, apart from those cemeteries which grew along the roads to the east of the Upper City (**68**).

Although the legal status of the suburbs remains uncertain (their occupants would have been enfranchised by the edict of Caracalla of 213), the changing extent of the settlement is a clue to economic prosperity, and the extra-mural areas are the principal source of information about both commercial activity and the population. Furthermore, at Lincoln it is the waterlogged low-lying land in the valley which contains almost all the evidence for organic materials and that regarding the environment. Each of the various areas is discussed in turn, with separate chapters devoted to the waterfront and the cemeteries.

The suburbs of the upper city

The evidence for legionary period occupation in the grounds of The Lawn to the west of the fortress has already been discussed. It is conceivable that there was not significant first-century settlement here but rather the early artefacts represent the later filling of early colonia pits – possibly stone quarries – with material derived from legionary rubbish dumps. Whether or not it came from these, stone would have been required both for the new front of the rampart and the range of public buildings being erected in the first half of the second century (chapter 6). Similar quarry pits were found to the rear of the western rampart at Westgate. Later in the second century a row of traders' houses developed along the south side of the street issuing from the west gate. There were presumably similar structures on the north side of the road, which further out may have followed a north-westerly course along the edge of the ridge or a route along its base. Stone quarries further west may have preceded the shops. The area to the north here is suggested above (p.72) as a possible site for the amphitheatre. Further south in the grounds of The Lawn, burials were discovered during the nineteenth century.

Both commercial occupation and burials were also to be found on the east side. Late second century and later commercial structures were discovered south of the road *c*.200m to the east of the gate, their standard of construction lower than that found elsewhere. They may have stood at the edge of that commercial zone. Beyond, cremations and inhumations extended for at least 800m further east, along the two principal roads now represented by Greetwell Road and Wragby Road (**68**).

To the north, a third-century commercial property, probably succeeding an earlier building, was found in 1995 *c*.50m outside the North Gate. Many graves came to light during the eighteenth and nineteenth centuries on both sides of Ermine Street, and extending well to the east. Structures found in the grounds of Bishop Grosseteste College, *c*.600m outside the walled area, appear to lie beyond the cemeteries (**25**), and are then more likely to have formed part of a rural establishment.

In summary, there was extensive development on all sides of the upper city from the second century, with commercial structures along the streets immediately outside, while areas beyond and to the rear were largely designated for burial grounds. The cemeteries are discussed further below in chapter 10.

The suburbs of the lower walled city

As with the upper city, settlement clustered principally along the roads which issued from the gates. Burials have been found both close to and at some considerable distance from the east and west gates (**68**). There was clearly use of the hillside's lower slopes for burial from an early date, continuing into the period when inhumation was introduced. As noted above, the area outside the east gate probably housed some fine monuments, later built into the city wall. The nearby site of Lincoln College also contained a second-century pottery kiln, probably one of several, and moulds indicating large-scale production of counterfeit silver coins in the early third century – when a dearth of small change meant that it became common for local issues to be manufactured.

Further south, there was more industrial occupation in the second century (pre-dating the construction of the defences). Adjacent to a furnace used for iron-smelting, a timber house was rebuilt in stone and a private bath suite added. The occupants' livelihood may subsequently have been affected by the building of the city wall. Remains of another establishment lay *c*.250m to the east of the gate; it included an east-west stone wall at least 9m long, almost too wide for the gable end of a simple trader's house.

As with the upper city, the suburbs to the east and west of the lower walled area contained a mixture of commercial/industrial properties and cemeteries, with detached rural establishments beyond the limits of settlement.

The southern suburb

Evidence for occupation to the south of the walled city is more substantial, and it has included examination of both the waterside (see chapter 9) and the extensive ribbon development further to the south. Its situation, taking in reclaimed former marshy ground, resembles the extensive ribbon development to the south of the Thames Bridge at Southwark, across from the walled area of Roman London. There is also a parallel here with Lyons, where the *colonia* was largely on the hilltop, and the trading settlement by the river.

At 181-3 High Street, on what had been an island in the river before a causeway was built, the early Roman timber structures fronting Ermine Street may have served the military; the artefactual material suggests a link with the legion rather than a native source. That there was trading in the first *colonia* structure here by *c*.AD 100 is clear from the fact that it produced coins of the previous decade. In a subsequent phase, the large number of pottery vessels used for pouring and imbibing suggests either a tavern (it had a cellar), or a more serious ritual. The ceramic collection from later second- and third-century structures reflects an apparent shift to dining as well

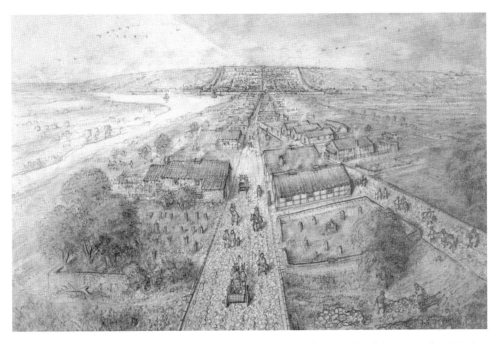

51 *Reconstruction drawing of traders' houses in the southern suburb, south of the point where Ermine Street and the Fosse Way diverged. D. Vale*

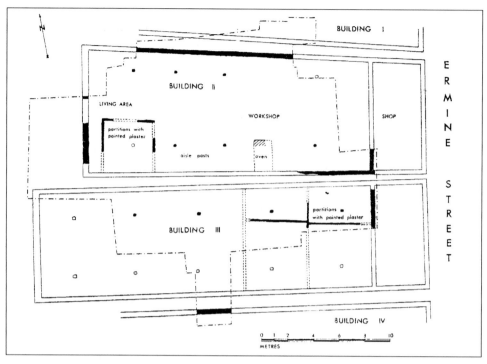

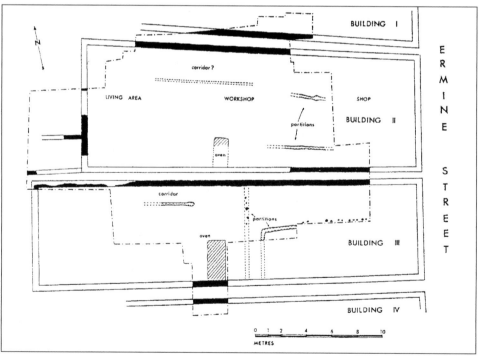

52 *Row of four traders' houses found beneath St Mark's Church (lower High Street), 1977. Upper drawing: early third century; lower drawing: late third century*

as drinking, associated with an unusual circular structure, perhaps a temple. It was only at a later stage that the site was used for industrial and commercial activity.

The land between this site and the river course to the north has been little explored. The land to its south included a southern arm of the river, and was too damp and low-lying for settlement until it was reclaimed. The higher land at Monson Street, beyond the postulated fork in the road system, had been used as a cemetery in the first century, but by the early second century there was industrial activity, including smithing, here as well as *c*.50m to the south. The combination of drier ground and an important roadside location would have been favourable for trading.

In the mid- to late second century, the marshy ground to the north was subsequently transformed into a major commercial suburb by a huge 'landfill' operation, undertaken either as a municipal or a private enterprise, but certainly under official control. It was a successful venture. By the early third century, ribbon development stretched for well to the south of the river (**51**). The largest single investigation of the sequence took place in 1976-7 at the former site of St Mark's Church. The land was first drained using a system of channels, whose fills produced waste from shoemaking. The ground level was then raised by about a metre to a similar level to the higher terrace. The first commercial structures against the main road may have been modest stalls. In the late second and early third century, a row of at least four adjacent traders' houses was constructed, each measuring *c*.8-9m wide and *c*.25-30m long. They were subsequently rebuilt, first with narrow stone walls, or at least sills, and later completely in stone (**52**). Until there were load-bearing stone walls, the roofs were supported principally by aisle posts. They had tile roofs, apart from one late building which used stone slates.

Their working areas were normally located in the central part of the building, behind the shop and in front of the living accommodation, and perhaps also in the yard to the rear. Access from the shop to the domestic quarters, and from the workshop to the rear yard, was provided along corridors adjacent to an outside wall. The buildings may have housed changing commercial uses, not easily discernible from the surviving fragmentary evidence of ovens (**53**), hearths, and possible vats. The heating and/or cooking of food, and metallurgical and other manufacturing crafts are likely to have featured prominently among the trades, but the waste products were not located: there may well have been clues in the rubbish dumps behind the buildings, but these unfortunately lay outside the excavated area.

Some surviving details were informative. A large stone with two bowl-shaped hollows had been set into a floor – it was possibly used to hold water or for standard measures (**54**): examples of table tops with similar depressions are known from Pompeii and Tivoli in Italy, and from Nyon in Switzerland. They were known as weighing-tables (*mensae ponderariae*) and were often set up in prominent positions such as adjacent to the forum. The stone from Lincoln was presumably in a secondary position, although it came from a building fairly early in the sequence.

Pottery vessels with representations of the smith-god, a phallic-shaped pot and a face-pot from a third-century phase are considered to indicate a household shrine for a blacksmith. Evidence for the waste products of smithing, in the form of hammer-

53 *One of the ovens found in a trader's house at the St Mark's Church site*

scale, was found at various of the houses in the suburb. In the fourth century, individual pots were buried in the successive floors against a wall, probably to keep cash safely, or to hold water or even urine. Two still had lids in position. In another phase there may have been a different use: rooms immediately behind the shop front were decorated and one contained a phallic object. The provision of a decorated suite towards the street end, rather than at the rear, appears to signal a change to a trade giving priority to receiving guests.

The sequence of rebuildings, to a similar pattern but at different times, may suggest that the traders sooner or later owned their houses, while other rebuildings may have been occasioned by fires. The pottery from the site would suggest that the apogee of these houses was in the late third to early fourth centuries. Some houses were abandoned by *c*.370, but others continued in occupation, or were reoccupied, until almost the end of the Roman period. A decline in building standards is discernible in the latest phases, when habitation was confined to the eastern part of the houses. By this date, the ground level had been again raised, presumably against the rising river level.

The boundaries between these houses did not shift here. Less than 100m to the south, however, a mid- to late second-century timber house, which had stood to the north of an east-west watercourse, shifted wall lines after the stream or drain was backfilled; presumably it was diverted. The replacement buildings straddled the former boundary. Iron hammer-scale was associated with the earlier building, and fragments of a smith-god pot found on later deposits may be residual, but certainly another of these buildings was occupied by a smith. Imported marble veneers found later in the sequence could have been incorporated into the structure.

Of the twenty or so traders' houses now known in this suburb, the most southerly found to date were those to the north and south of Monson Street, fronting on to Ermine Street to the east as well as to the Fosse Way on the west (**51**). Some of the buildings had painted walls and stone roof slates. Fragments of a ceramic figure of a god – a household god? – dated to the mid- to late third century. The third-century pottery from one house, also associated with copper-working, included high-status dining vessels, while the adjacent building produced more of a concentration of kitchen wares: the contrast might simply reflect the different functions of those rooms investigated.

No site to the south of the junction of High Street and Sibthorp Street has been the subject of modern excavations, but this area may have been zoned for burial (chapter 10). A recent re-examination by David Stocker of a stone sculpture incorporated into the eleventh-century tower of the Church of St Peter at Gowts, on the south side of Sibthorp Street, has speculated that it represents the Mithraic god Arimanius, and as such is evidence for a temple of Mithras in the city. Such temples were most commonly found in the second century associated with former legionaries, but located at the settlement fringe and close to water; the location is accordingly appropriate and the stone need not have been moved far.

Evidence for the use of land to the rear of the street frontages was obtained at Chaplin Street, where second- to third-century features parallel to the main street may indicate either drainage or agricultural activity. However, we understand too little of how or whether the land here was drained.

54 *Stone set into the floor of one of the workshops at the St Mark's Church site. The depressions cut into the stone are similar to those used for standard measures, but here may simply have held water*

Communications: roads, rivers, canals and water supply

The presence of a legion in the city had ensured good communications: the construction of both Ermine Street – possibly replacing a prehistoric route way along the edge of the ridge – and the Fosse Way belong to this period. Tillbridge Lane, the route deviating north-westwards from Ermine Street *c*.5km north of Lincoln, was probably also of military origin. It provided a route to Doncaster which involved a crossing of the Trent at Marton and Littleborough and of the Idle east of Bawtry (**60**).

This military road system was consolidated with the foundation of the *colonia*. Roads to the coast, and southwards to the east of Sleaford (Mareham Lane), may belong to this secondary development, since they do not appear to link military bases or their early civilian successors. Drury noted the need for a causeway across the marshy ground: the Fosse Way and Ermine Street converged at the point where the higher terrace ended, at the start of the causeway, which Drury described as 'concreted', i.e. with mortar between the stones (**2**). Whether the concrete was a surface or make-up was not clear. It is presumed that the army had constructed some sort of embankment or causeway over the damper ground, but the more solid construction appears to belong to the *colonia* period, possibly connected with the development of the suburb. The section of road exposed beneath St Mary's Guildhall suggests that the surface of pebbles was mortared in the mid-Roman period (**55**), and

55 *Third-century road surface (Fosse Way) found beneath the Norman St Mary's Guildhall, 1982. Note the wheel ruts*

there are other examples within the city of this type of construction. The later surfaces at most sites were of larger pebbles, while the main street of the city was paved. Since even major streets can be so much less substantial outside the settlements, it is no wonder that we cannot yet determine the precise line of Ermine Street in the South Common area.

In the later third and fourth centuries, milestones became a common feature along major roads, partly for propaganda. At Lincoln, that of Victorinus (AD 268-70) was adjacent to the forum in the centre of the upper city (*RIB* 2241) (**32**). A second almost certainly stood at the edge of the Fosse Way a modern mile to the south of the forum, but less than one Roman mile from the south gate of the lower city. The third-century inscription to Valerianus (*RIB* 2240) was found some time ago nearby, but only represents the top of the stone. The square-sectioned base of the milestone, and a large hole in the Roman road in which it had been set, were found at St Mary's Guildhall.

At this location, the Fosse Way was *c*.7-8m wide with a central drain, and the Ermine Street, also with a drain, perhaps a little narrower, was apparently surfaced with paving stones. Wheel ruts were visible on the stretch of the third-century Fosse Way excavated (and now exposed within the building; **55**). In his new book on Roman roads, Hugh Davies suggests that the use of gravel eased the strain on vehicles. Limestone blocks have been noted at several locations, including on Ermine Street north of Lincoln, where the road was roughly 6m wide but on an embankment perhaps twice that size. The possible layout of roads issuing from other city gates is shown on **25**. Some can only be plotted with certainty for a short distance but may have extended much further.

If roads required considerable investment, canals were even more expensive, but once built would greatly facilitate the movement of heavy goods. The date of the creation of the Fossdyke canal is commonly presumed to have been in the second century, but its Roman origin cannot be proven at present. Its construction involved the canalisation of two river courses: the Till, which flows into the western end of Brayford Pool, and the extinct stream which flows east from the Trent at Torksey. To effect the link between the Witham and the Trent, a new cutting was required only between Odder and Drinsey Nook. The finding of a bronze statuette in the canal at Torksey has been adduced as evidence for a Roman date (**colour plate 29**), but given the pre-existence of a watercourse here, this find is slender evidence, and equally so for the various other Roman finds discovered. Apart from other factors such as availability of brushwood and clay, some of the pottery kilns around the Roman city would have been well placed to make use of the Fossdyke, but the existence of the River Till may have been just as useful. It may be more significant that pottery made in the Trent Valley and fine wares from northern Britain (like Crambeck Ware) do not appear in any quantity at Lincoln. An Anglo-Scandinavian date may then be more likely for the canal. On the other hand, the large columns of the forum and some architectural fragments re-used in the city wall were of millstone grit, and the existence of the canal would have considerably facilitated the transport of these heavy blocks from the Pennines via the Trent. Presumably, the large blocks of Lincolnshire limestone used for the so-called 'screen of the gods', a monumental arch in London, were moved down the Witham and around the coast.

The Car Dyke, which deviates from the Witham *c.*4km east of Lincoln, is certainly a Roman feature, but doubts remain about its function. It extends from near Peterborough to Lincoln, and served either as a canal or as a drain, or more probably as both.

Unlike several Roman legionary fortresses and towns, Lincoln was not sufficiently close to the sea to accommodate sea-going vessels, in spite of the fact that the coast, or more accurately the shoreline, lay much nearer in the Roman period. It was normal for goods to be moved to river-going vessels before being transported inland. A site which may have served for trans-shipment has been identified at Adlingfleet on the Humber Estuary.

The aqueduct

The Lincoln aqueduct was one of most impressive and technologically sophisticated of Roman civic water supply systems in Britain, but is at the same time one of the least understood. A pipeline encased in waterproof concrete, running adjacent and

56 *Section of the aqueduct revealed during development in 1973, off Nettleham Road*

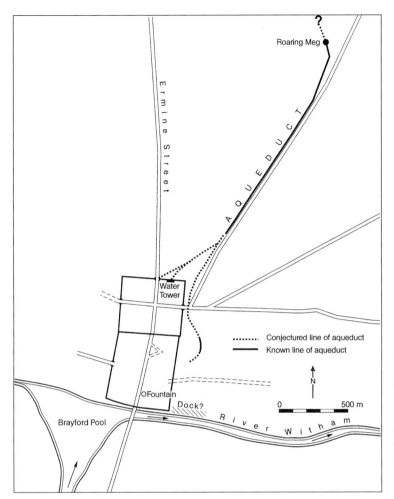

57 *Map of the known line of the aqueduct. Neither its source, nor its route close to the city, are known for certain. Other elements of the water supply are indicated*

parallel to Nettleham Road, north-east of the city, has been known for *c*.300 years (**56** & **57**). The investigations of 1951-2 by Hugh Thompson produced evidence for a bridged structure close to the suspected source, the Roaring Meg spring. This being over 20m lower than the site of the upper city, it required an effective method by which water might be raised. Initially, a force-pump was favoured. In the absence of unequivocal evidence, there has been much informed speculation about how water reached the city through the closed pipe system. Certainly, the force-pump is no longer seen as practicable, and some authorities actually speculate on the possibility that the system ever worked; certainly there is little trace of lime-scale inside the pipe. The general consensus (although by no means universally accepted) is now that the source was at a higher level and further north, and the system was the so-called 'inverted siphon'. There are certainly good precedents for bringing water to the town from a considerable distance – for instance at Cologne and Lyons. Some progress may be possible in the near future, first by investigating the field to the north of Roaring Meg for any continuation of the pipeline, and if this proves positive, by searching for a source along the Jurassic Ridge to the north of the city. There are indications of the pipeline, for instance, in the parish of Burton, only 3km from the city on the west side of Ermine Street.

As yet there is no evidence that the pipeline extended beyond Roaring Meg. If this was the source, a lifting device using buckets and chains might have been provided here. Some argue that the foundations exposed were too insubstantial to carry a tower 20m high, even a timber one, but this is not necessarily true. A bucket and chain system for raising water has recently been found in London, and it is possible that a similar system could have been employed at Lincoln for the final lift into the city, at a point still to be determined: tracing the course of the aqueduct as it approached the walled area is another priority (**57**).

The capacity of the single pipeline found to date could have coped with the demands of the public baths, but probably not much beyond. There may have been other pipes – one was noted on Greestone Stairs, perhaps heading for the public fountain – but the civic authorities were also capable of digging wells such as that in the forum. Spring water was favoured if it could be obtained, and the hillside contained several possible sources.

The urban fringe and the rural interface

The city drew many of its supplies, from raw materials to food and manufactured goods, from its rural hinterland, some from very close to the city. Exploitation of natural resources at the edge of town, and the industrial activity which they supported, were essential to the urban economy. There are some data on this topic, but less about the organisation of the city's agricultural hinterland. There was a close relationship, socially as well as economically, between the town and the surrounding countryside: the leading citizens lived for much of the time on rural estates, the source of their wealth. Farmland close to the city may even have been run from urban residences.

Lincoln's situation on the Jurassic ridge has meant that its site has been a source of building stone since the Roman period. The city was constructed largely out of local limestone, probably obtained from adjacent quarries. Some embellishments came from a greater distance, including the sandstone columns of the forum, and certain luxuries from even further afield: luxury marble veneers were obtained from various sources around the Mediterranean – a feature common to several cities in Roman Britain.

Geological analysis of the city walls identified various local limestones. The true oolitic stone, including the 'Ancaster' freestone, was not among them. Although good stone had been used as early as the first century for the large blocks required for legionary tombstones, the stone from the better beds at the local quarries was not employed on the wall until the rebuilding from the mid- to late Roman period. Outcrops on the western and southern scarps of the Ridge may have been the first areas to be exploited since they were so accessible. Immediately inside and outside

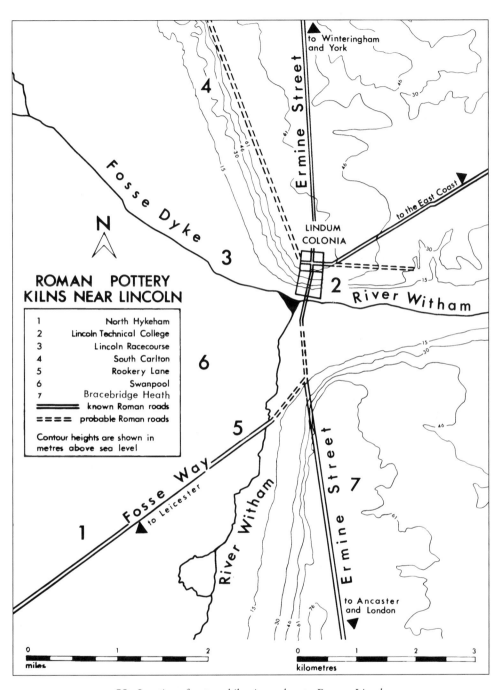

58 *Location of pottery kilns in or close to Roman Lincoln*

the western defences on the hilltop, there were pits of various sizes which appear to be quarries. Some had presumably provided stone for the first stone fortifications and public buildings.

The mortars used in the city wall have also been analysed. There was a distinction between the gravel used for the earlier and later walls. This suggested different sources, the earlier source probably lying along the rivers to the south and west of the walled city (including along the course of the River Till/Fossdyke). The source for the later wall was further to the south-west, the same area of the city – Boultham and Swanpool – where the major pottery industry of the third and fourth centuries was also situated.

The various kilns of the local pottery industry were mostly located on the urban fringe (**58**), but in some cases several kilometres away. The earliest so far found, dated to *c*.AD 90-110, was at North Hykeham, *c*.7km to the south-west. Its repertoire included pots in rustic ware, but few have been found in the city. A mid- to late second-century industry was situated on the scarp at South Carlton, a similar distance to the north-west. It numbered military garrisons in the north among its main clients. While these kilns may have owed their location to their clay sources, others could be related rather to ease of transport to market. The industry based at the former Racecourse site, on the western edge of the modern city, was close to the River Till/Fossdyke. That producing stamped *mortaria* (spouted mixing-bowls) of Vitalis was close to the walled town, but Vitalis' products found their way to army bases further west and north.

The Swanpool industry appears to originate from an existing regional or tribal tradition, developed to serve the needs of the city and surrounding hinterland. (There were other large industries close to Lincoln in the Trent valley and in and around Market Rasen.) The Swanpool manufacturing centre survived almost to the end of the Roman period, for as long as the city provided a market. The kiln types resemble some already in use in the Lincoln area, suggesting that the potters were locally-based. Whether the industry moved to this site because suitable clay was discovered in the course of gravel quarrying, or vice versa, we cannot say. The presence of iron slag in the Swanpool mortaria might even suggest that iron-working was taking place nearby. David Stocker has pointed out the close correlation between the locations of kiln sites and exposed clay next to the waterways.

The only local tile kiln identified to date also had a rural situation, close to the Car Dyke, south-east of the city, in Heighington parish (**59**). Land and taxation costs were presumably lower for rural sites, fuel in the form of coppiced wood could be close by, and out of the city the resulting air pollution would be reduced. A third-century kiln found close to Ermine Street at Bracebridge Heath, to the south of the Witham gap, may have belonged to the settlement in that area.

The boundary between urban land use and the start of rural occupation is discernible in places. The two stone buildings adjacent to Ermine Street, *c*.600m to the north of the city, were located immediately beyond land containing burials, and as such might be considered to be outside the urban limits. Occupation here appears to have intensified from the mid-second century, but it did not last beyond the mid-

59 *The tile-kiln excavated in Heighington parish, south-east of Lincoln and close to the Car Dyke, in 1976*

fourth. The evidence of the pottery, with a good number of fine wares and imports, suggests a degree of prosperity and status. The environmental evidence provides clues as to function: the range of molluscs indicates that it was located in a mixed environment, in open land with some shade, and there were traces of cereal grains and of spelt wheat. From the occurrence of the bones of neonates among the sheep and cattle we can deduce that some were kept and bred.

This may have formed part of a villa estate, or simply a farm serving the town. In the southern suburb, land to the rear of traders' houses was used for small-scale agriculture. The nearest definite villa to the city was on the north side of the Witham Valley *c.*2km east of the walls, towards Greetwell, at a point which gave excellent views both over and down the valley. Its remains were most impressive, but were discovered and then largely destroyed by late nineteenth-century mining operations. The paintings of the villa's plan and decoration made by the Resident Manager of the ironstone quarry were of some skill (**colour plates 12** & **14**), while brief accounts made by those who visited the site could still note its opulence and the quality of the mosaics and the painted wall-plaster, including the figure of a swallow and a floral design (**colour plate 8**). The recent re-examination of records of the mosaic pavements by David Neal has suggested that, even among the high-quality mosaics found in north Lincolnshire (though not so much in the city), Greetwell Villa has produced examples of the finest. The length of the corridors (the east-west pavilion measuring all of 86m), and the use of techniques which could only be undertaken by continental mosaicists, add up to a palatial site, rare in Britain. No illustrations survive of the northern range, where the main residence was probably situated, and we have no stratigraphical information or sealed dating evidence, but the style of the decoration and the coin series from the site indicate occupation during the fourth century, lasting to the end of the Roman period (chapter 12). Was it merely the villa of a very wealthy and ostentatious citizen, or rather the palace of the fourth-century provincial governor?

Most villas were grand country residences for the local aristocracy, designed to impress, which also formed estate centres: great wealth was only normally available through landholding. They were farming establishments where grain was produced, processed, and stored before delivery to town. Several sumptuous examples are known within a few miles of the city, especially on the Lincoln Edge overlooking the valley to the west, close to Burton, Glentworth and Scampton. These all lay to the north of the city, but a similar pattern might be expected to the south, and the pavement found beneath the church at Canwick, on the south side of the gap, betrays the location of the nearest of these to the city. Like that at Norton Disney to the east of the Fosse Way, south-west of Lincoln, they had good communication links, being situated close to a main route (**60**). Some estates near to Lincoln would both have formed the main residences of the colonists who served as the city's magistrates, and have provided their principal source of income.

Another, less aristocratic, settlement lay to the north-east of the Greetwell Villa, and immediately outside the line of the former triple ditch system. It contained a rectilinear pattern of field boundaries, within which were some structures identified from samples as grain stores, as well as corn dryers and stone-lined drains. There was also a small inhumation cemetery, dating from the mid-third century AD, aligned on one of the north-south ditches. Similar features were detected further south by a geophysical survey, and it may therefore have been part of the nearby villa estate. Further east, along the river towards Fiskerton, aerial photography has revealed at least two features which may represent temples, perpetuating the religious signifi-cance of the valley. To the north-west of the walled city, remains of stone buildings and associated inhumations dated to the third century were found on Long Leys Road at the base of the hill. These may have belonged to the Burton Villa estate, which in turn may have had its origins in the Iron Age cliff-top settlement (p.29), but such a prime location might be expected to have lain within the *territorium* which is discussed below.

Town and country relationships

This is a book about an urban centre in a period when about 90 per cent of the population lived and worked in the countryside. As we have seen, much of the surrounding land was organised to serve its needs. The city was not only a consumer of rural produce, but also provided a market for other local and imported products,

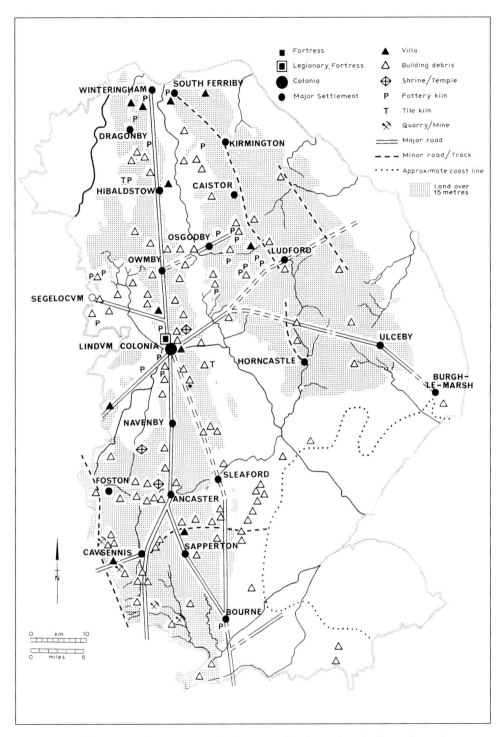

60 *Map of Roman settlements in Lincolnshire; note the relationship of villas to the road system*

and itself offered goods and services. Some evidence has been set out above on how the countryside immediately around Lincoln might have related to the city. This relationship changed over time. The evidence for farming already noted demonstrates the contribution which can be made by environmental evidence, including animal bones. The much greater sample of bones from the Waterside sites (p.111) still represents only a small part of the city. Apart from meat, other requirements of the town-dwellers included fuel, fruit and vegetables, beer and wine, wool and leather for clothing, and herbs and flowers.

Central to our understanding is the economic inter-relationship of the various levels (the hierarchy) of settlements, which can be addressed partly by tracing the sources of materials found in the city. Some information on nearby 'small towns' or 'market centres' is already available: at Ancaster, on nearby sites along the Fosse Way, on the sites to the north of Lincoln, and on small towns in eastern Britain more generally (**60**). It is not within the scope of this book to describe the various urban and other nucleated settlements in the region around Lincoln. Many originated in the Iron Age. They varied from large 'villages' and roadside agglomerations to walled areas with some evidence of internal planning and official function, but most served as markets for their own agricultural hinterlands. In turn, each of these too had a changing economic relationship with Lincoln itself, as both customers and producers, and many market centres grew considerably, especially in the third and fourth centuries. Lincoln in the meantime shows no signs of having lost its commercial vigour to these smaller centres, but its special status, first as a *colonia*, then in the late Roman period as a provincial capital (chapter 11), may have strengthened its position.

It will be some time before we can document with any certainty the speed and effect of the Roman occupation on the countryside. There will have to be analysis of dated artefacts from the 'hinterland' in order to understand how far from the city its products penetrated. That distance will vary according to the different materials and through time, and each tribal area may have functioned differently.

The *territorium*

The above problem is to some extent connected with the *territorium*: land which lay directly under the control of the *colonia*, as distinct from what is meant by the economic hinterland. The *territorium* might have corresponded closely to that controlled during the military occupation, including the *prata legionis* discussed above, but whether it can be defined is more problematic, since it may have left no traces. In Italy and some Mediterranean provinces such lands were 'centuriated', divided into areas of standard size (normally squares 2,400 Roman feet long), and some would argue that similar land division would have been undertaken for the early military colonies in Britain. This characteristic was becoming less standard by the mid-second century. Lincoln's case (and that of Gloucester) would accordingly be marginal. It may even have been true that the countryside around Lincoln was already intensively farmed, and the existing field systems were maintained, but under different authority.

Several researchers have spent many years looking for evidence of centuriation in Britain, but none has come forward with evidence for the Lincoln area which deserved to be scrutinised until recent years. Mr A. Syme, a retired engineer from Leicester, and Dr J.W. Peterson of the University of East Anglia, at roughly the same time, both proposed that the alignment of fields to the north and south of the city derives from their Roman layout. These fields follow the alignment of the coast road (Wragby Road) issuing from the east gate. It will prove difficult to subject these hypotheses to formal scrutiny, in that dating them is well-nigh impossible. Any new layout (*limitatio*) would be expected to date to the period soon after the designation of the *territorium*, in this case by the early second century. Recent work at West Deeping, which though well to the south of Lincoln would fall within the area suggested by Peterson to be centuriated, indicated major reorganisation in the second century. There was certainly some expansion into the fens, perhaps subsequently curtailed by the later Roman rise in sea level.

On the basis of Italian parallels, Ian Richmond considered that the *territorium* would have covered an area of not less than 100 square miles, including land along the ridge and more in 'the marshes', but a smaller area is possible. The land in the Fens adjacent to the Car Dyke is one favoured candidate: recent research confirms that major engineering works, including canals and roads, were undertaken from the late first century and that there was intensified settlement from the Roman period. The definition of the exact area might prove to be beyond our reach, but one indication may be the distribution of settlements, milestones, temples, etc., which seem

61 *Inscription to* Mars Rigonemetos *and to the* Numina Augustorum, *from a shrine at Nettleham, c.3km north-east of the Roman city*

105

to imply some dependence on Lincoln. Sites such as the shrine at Nettleham jointly dedicated to *Mars Rigonemetos* and the *Numina Augustorum* (**61**) must lie within the boundary (p.142). Another idea is that sites noted on the milestones, including Littleborough-on-Trent, with distances measured to them from Lincoln, also lay within the territory. Analysis of the sources of the stones used for the milestones suggested that, if the *colonia* had been responsible for their provision, Lincoln's *territorium* was even more extensive than many expected.

9 On the waterfront

The land adjacent to the river was an important focus (**62**). The river would have been much used for transporting materials, probably in flat-bottomed barge-type vessels suitable for river trade: even though the coast was much closer, trans-shipment from seagoing vessels is now considered likely for an inland location like Lincoln. Presumably, there was considerable overseas trade, including the wine from south-west France whose export was organised by M. Aurelius Lunaris. The waterfront, with its warehouses and wet deposits, is obviously a crucial element in our under-standing of the topography, environment, and commercial life of the city, but it is only in recent decades that this fact has been generally appreciated. Its potential should have been clear much earlier. The timber piles of a pre-Norman bridge or causeway, and the huge stonework of a north-south wall which might have been the east side of a dock, were both observed by Michael Drury as long ago as 1887-8, close to St Benedict's Church, to the south of the present High Bridge. Two stone 'waterwheel hubs' from in the river adjacent to High Bridge are now re-interpreted as part of a road-rammer or as columns which adorned a Roman bridge. A more convincing candidate for a dock or quay came to light further downstream, imme-diately to the east of the lower walled city, in 1954, even though it lay c.80m to the north of the present river line. A 6m-long stretch of stone wall, running east-west with a return northwards at its western end, was recorded by Hugh Thompson during the construction of the telephone exchange at the junction of Broadgate and St Rumbold Street.

Excavations close to the waterfront since the 1970s, and in particular those in 1987-91 at Waterside North, have demonstrated that at least 50m and in places up to 100m have been reclaimed on various banks since the Roman period. The position of the dock found in 1954 is therefore consistent with the emerging evidence for the line of the river. It is notable that, apart from those remains recorded by Drury and by Thompson, no major waterfront features of the Roman period have been found – rather there was a shelving 'beach' or fenced bank, possibly provided with occasional slipways and/or jetties.

The first waterfront sites to be investigated were adjacent to the Brayford Pool. Work on the north side of the Pool, near to its north-east corner, made it clear that in the early Roman period the Pool had extended much of the way to the city defences. About 200m further west, the site of what is now the Courtyard Hotel lay within the pool, with sandy and peaty deposits suggesting an environment of dry land surrounded by ponds, pools and streams. On the east shore of the Pool, the waterside was perhaps as far as 100m from its present line, closer to the line of

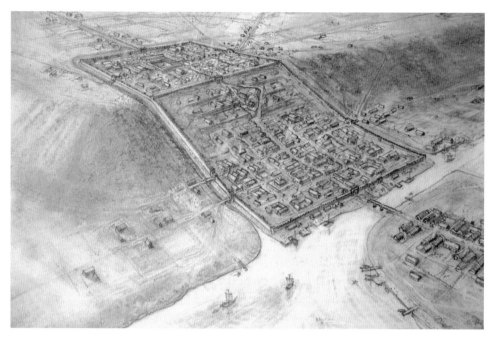

62 *Reconstruction drawing of the Roman city and the riverfront, with the dock shown to the east of the walled area.* D. Vale

Ermine Street (High Street) than to the present Brayford. Its position was more precisely defined in subsequent excavations. It was at least 75m away during the second century, but was advanced by 22m during the third century by means of a series of dumps held back by a row of timber stakes. There was evidence here to suggest that peat accumulated in the shallows, as in the earlier phase, but that the water's edge may also have been exploited for trapping fish. Further dumping to raise the bank level took place in the fourth century, possibly to counter a rise in river level, and the river front was advanced by a further 15m or so.

The third-century dumps contained organic finds, such as leather sandals, as well as animal bones, and some informative groups of pottery: in particular, the fine wares contained a high proportion of table and drinking vessels, and a relatively high proportion of samian ware from Gaul. One suggested interpretation of the occurrence of these imports is that a nearby site may have been used for trans-shipment for a while, or was it close to a trader's premises specialising in such imports? There was at least one tavern or other establishment nearby where liquids were imbibed.

At St Benedict's Square, close to Brayford Head, the earliest waterfront investigated was of the third century: it appeared to be a bank with horizontal posts incorporated, perhaps for stability, but also for mooring small boats. Again there was later dumping to facilitate reclamation and indications of a hard-standing; a drainage channel running roughly east-west suggests that the waterfront was then established on a more north-south alignment. It was just to the north of here that Drury had noted the wall of a possible dock.

Apart from the structural evidence, and the abundance of artefacts contained in the reclamation dumps, the sites also preserved considerable quantities of other organic materials. These indicate much more than the range of goods traded. Analysis of the diatoms (single-celled algae) and molluscs found species consistent with the idea that the river flow varied through time, possibly as a result of human influence: Roman sluices upstream, and intensification of agriculture, may have increased run-off. David Stocker has suggested that controls may have been installed downstream to ensure that the Witham remained navigable despite a rise in sea level. There was an apparent rise of 1-2m in the river level, to *c*.4m, during the Roman period, which may reflect that of the sea level, but could alternatively have been due to artificial agency. It may have required the replacement of some of the sloping hard-standings with vertical wharves.

The reclamation schemes may have served also to create a deeper water channel. There is a great deal more that we still have to learn about operations on the river. For instance, canalisation of the watercourses upstream may have formed part of a scheme to facilitate navigation, including both the Witham, and the River Till west of Lincoln. The raising of the river level might also have been motivated by the need to create a navigable canal link – the Fossdyke – to the Trent, but as we have noted above, the construction date of this canal is still to be determined. (The Sincil Dyke, which forms an artificial channel to the east of the structures in the southern suburb, is now regarded as a medieval feature.)

The riverside east of Brayford Pool: recent investigations

The results of the investigations on the site of the Waterside Shopping Centre provided much enlightenment about the environment and the economy. It was not a simple picture. The water's edge, probably slow-moving shallows choked with rushes, was advanced southwards with dumps of rubbish, interspersed with naturally-forming peat deposits. What appeared to be a foreshore was formed of stone and coarse sand (mortar?) and revetted by vertical piles. Flowing past it from the hillside was a channel containing wood fragments and many artefacts, which had remained open to the mid-fourth century. After this date, there was further reclamation. To the east along the river, a fourth-century shelving beach was identified, later being buried as the riverfront was further advanced. Adjacent to the Ermine Street bridge, there were indications that the waterfront here lay further south. From the late third century, metalled surfaces sloped down both southwards and eastwards, presumably deviating from the road. They may have led not to a wharf but to a nearby ford. Platforms or piers ran both eastwards from Ermine Street and southwards from the road outside the city wall, with shallow inlets adjacent, subject to seasonal flooding. Boats may have beached here, along jetties. It is possible that this part of the water-front remained largely marginal to the main docks downstream, but new arrange-ments might have been made, following the construction of a sluice, which could have involved more substantial waterfront structures to house larger boats.

63 *A wooden paddle-shaped object from the Waterside North excavations; possibly a shovel for a bread oven*

These rubbish dumps used as the basis for the later reclamation were rich in artefacts and organic material, many of them brought here from other sites in the city. They contained large numbers of domestic objects, as well as evidence for commercial and industrial activity (**colour plate 25**). The coins were almost entirely late Roman in date, with a concentration in the mid-fourth century but extending to the 370s–80s. How far they are indicative of commercial transactions being undertaken at the waterside is difficult to know: as was common in this period, the vast majority were of low value, probably used for cash transactions until lost or discarded. Notable among other finds were some enigmatic wooden objects (**63**), over seventy leather shoes (**colour plate 21**), and off-cuts from leatherworking. A wooden writing tablet with a recessed panel (**64**) and nineteen writing pens or *styli* (**65**), which could be used for writing in wax, may have been used in conjunction. Together with the balance, these could be adduced as evidence for commercial and bureaucratic activity as goods were brought in or taken away by the boats. Other objects included jewellery and glass, and even fragments of armour and weapons. How many of these were much earlier in date than the dumps is uncertain: the late dating of the coins is a clue, and it seems more likely that the reclamation operations were limited to a few major schemes.

64 *Wooden writing tablet, with recessed panel for wax, from the Waterside North site*

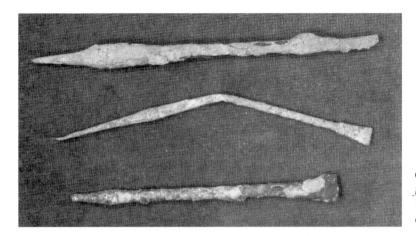

65 *Iron styli from the Waterside North excavations*

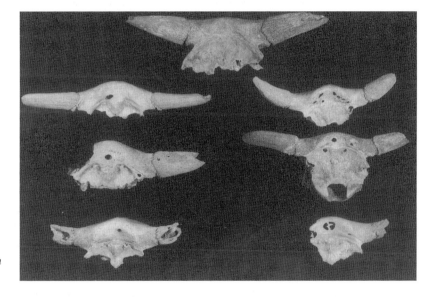

66 *Cattle skulls with perforations possibly caused by pressure from the yoke*

The collection of animal bones provides information on the quality of stock of different species and their relative frequency, numbers of wild as opposed to domestic animals, butchery practices, and diet. The most notable collection was that of fourth-century cattle, which has been interpreted as indicating butchery on a civic scale. There were vast numbers of mandibles and shoulders of beef used essentially as hardcore, dumped while they were still fairly fresh. Two types of butchery operation were noted: marrow extraction for lamps and cosmetics, and de-fleshing and dismemberment of joints for cheaper cuts of meat, as well as to provide shoulders for smoking. The cattle slaughtered were of moderate age and had probably been used for various purposes, including as draught animals, before being brought into market from outside the town (**66**).

There were also sheep, mainly but not exclusively kept for wool: most of the bones were of animals more than three years old. In addition, pigs, chickens and even dogs formed part of the diet. Other mammals found included hare, red and roe deer, and black rat. Among the bird bones from the city were cranes as well as geese and ducks. The fish species at Waterside North included the earliest (to date) British examples of carp and bitterling. A concentrated group of sand-eel bones is thought to represent either residue from manufacture of a local variant of *garum* (a Roman fish sauce), or the processing of larger species for which sand-eel were prey or bait.

Equally interesting, both from the point of view of the site and the river environment generally, were the insect remains. The presence of, for instance, a cockroach (again the earliest find from Britain) implies heated buildings, possibly for storing grain (this is a location where warehouses might be expected). This might suggest continuing organisation of the food supply into the late fourth century. Some insect remains may have been associated with manure from stables, suggesting that horses were still being quartered here. The insects are also informative regarding river conditions: they indicate largely still or sluggish water, and areas of stagnant pools in a river of low to moderate energy flow. The same impression is given by the sediments and the molluscan and diatom analysis. The picture is filled out by the evidence of plant remains, which suggest rich and varied vegetation. Many species were associated with wetland or marshland, and they included a number of crops as well as grasslands and damp meadows upstream, as well as weeds in the town. The nearby rural landscape was essentially an open one. The river at Lincoln was a basically freshwater environment, with occasional hints of tidal influence. The waterfront has much still to tell us about many aspects of life in the Roman city.

10 The places of the dead

From the time of their earliest traditions, the Romans disposed of the dead outside the city boundaries. It was a practice which conveniently disposed of the potential health risks as well as meeting the need for appropriate rituals. The dead may have been out of sight, but they were not necessarily out of mind. At the time of the conquest of Britain, cremation was universal, often with grave goods. During the Roman occupation of Britain, there was a gradual change to the practice of inhumation, burial of uncremated remains. Containers of various materials – or none – were used, up to large mausolea. At Lincoln, it appears that particular zones were designated for cemeteries, always outside the walled areas, and often beyond the commerical zones outside the gates (**25 & 68**).

The existence of cemeteries was noted by eighteenth-century antiquarians just as Lincoln was beginning to expand again and adjacent stone quarries were coming back into operation. Many finds of both cremations and inhumations came to light, producing large numbers of grave goods for museum collections. Tombstones and other monuments were more occasional discoveries (**colour plate 2**). The records of these discoveries are of value in establishing the location, date and burial rite, and in some cases the individuals involved, but little thought was given at the time to the potential of the information residing in the human remains found. The cemetery sites were located on the fringe of the modern town centre, beneath a relatively shallow accumulation of later deposits; there is little probability that much survives to be re-examined today or found in future. Those burials discovered during stone-quarrying, to the north and east of the upper city, have been totally destroyed.

The documentation of the early discoveries and their study can be summarised chronologically (see also chapter 1). William Stukeley noted the position of some of the cemeteries to the south, east and north-east of the Roman town when preparing a map of Lincoln in 1722. What he wrongly identified as three burial mounds or barrows which were still surviving at that time in the so-called 'Greetwell Fields', are now considered to represent remnants of late or post-medieval windmills. There were other 'burial places' close to Nettleham and Wragby Roads. Several later antiquarians contributed to the picture of which Richmond was able to summarise knowledge in 1946. By that date, the legionary-period cemeteries in the Monson Street and South Common areas had been located, as well as other finds on all sides of the city walls, as far out as the late first-century barrow at Riseholme, *c.*3km north of the city. More recent discoveries have included burials, revealed, ironically, during the digging of graves, in the modern Newport Cemetery (!); fragments of a re-used tombstone from the foundations of the medieval church of St Mark's in Wigford, possibly referring to

113

67 *Two fragments of a tombstone built into the foundations of St Mark's church possibly recording a town councillor (decurio)*

a *decurio* (**67**); another behind the northern defences at East Bight recording an inscription by two sons to their father; to the west of the lower city at Orchard Street, which produced a relief of Mother Goddesses (**84**), and, most importantly, an excavation at Monson Street in 1982, on the site of the first-century cemetery.

The map of current knowledge of all cemetery locations (**68**) probably indicates the approximate extent of the main cemeteries. Most lay close to the major roads issuing from the city, but there was an overflow into land in the north-east quadrant, between Newport, Nettleham Road, Wragby Road and Greetwell Road, as well as in parts of the hillside. They absorbed large tracts of extra-mural land not used for official or commercial buildings, and were generally beyond the commercial zones. It has been calculated that, for a city with an estimated population of 10,000, an average 350 burials would take place each year. In Lincoln's case, assuming a smaller

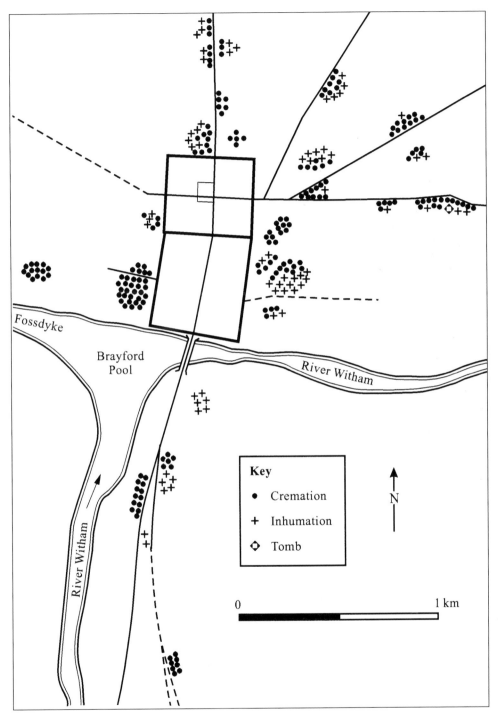

68 *Map showing the known extent of the cemeteries of Roman Lincoln*

population (which may be an underestimate), there would have been at least 50,000 individuals buried during the Roman period, but not all of them would necessarily have received a formal burial. The general impression is that burial location and practice at Lincoln was fairly orderly, typical of the major towns of Roman Britain. The change from cremation to inhumation took place at Lincoln during the third century, in line with the general trend for the province. The belief systems involved, details of burial rites, and the reasons for this empire-wide change in practice, are not discussed here for reasons of space.

At Lincoln, the early cemeteries south of the river continued to be used to some extent in the second and third centuries, although parts of them were swallowed up by the burgeoning commercial suburbs. The cremations from Monson Street have been mentioned above (chapter 5); they included children and women, and the excavated site may have been close to the pyre site (*ustrinum*). There were traces of charcoal and soot when tombstones were found here in 1849. These excavations also revealed the north side of a stone building of comparatively early date which has been interpreted as a mausoleum, possibly also containing the mosaic found *c.*1845 while several north-south inhumations were noted nearby. More recently, other north-south burials have turned up: two were found in 1987 to the rear of the traders' houses across from St Mark's Station, and another in 1996 in the grounds of Bishop Grosseteste College. Stukeley considered that an area further south along High Street (here the Fosse Way) contained many 'funeral monuments'.

Most of the burials encountered to date have been cremations, but most ceme-teries also seem to have contained later inhumations: caution must however be exercised in identifying finds of inhumations as Roman, since the medieval city contained about fifty separate cemeteries, many in similar locations to Roman burials, and there were many others in the city. Some special characteristics deserve comment. In addition to the barrow at Riseholme, and the much more doubtful ones mentioned by Stukeley, there was another documented example outside the west gate of the lower city. There were also burials in lead coffins, in stone sarcophagi, in tile-lined coffins, and another subterranean mausoleum, to the east of the upper city. Richmond identified *loculi* (literally 'pigeon-holes') in Newport not far outside the north gate, which accommodated rows of burials belonging to a burial club. The discovery of the tombstone of C. Antistius Frontinus (*RIB* 247), a treasurer of a guild – probably for a burial club – is cited as evidence for such arrangements (p.143).

The impression conveyed is one of metropolitan and Mediterranean cultural influences, but this cannot be assumed. They might have been erected either by immigrant Romans or by those who aspired to a Roman identity: in those tribal areas away from the south-east such monuments were almost invariably associated with incomers. The cosmopolitan nature of that part of the population whose apparent existence is archaeologically visible is reinforced by the inscriptions on many tombstones, including that belonging to Flavius Helius, a Greek (*RIB* 251). Like the legionaries (p.37), the *origines* of some *colonia* citizens were widely scattered.

Finds of infant remains have become a common phenomenon in Lincoln, as elsewhere, and especially from extra-mural traders' houses. Of the fourteen examples found in the southern suburb, all had died in the late foetal or perinatal periods (**69**). As a result, we cannot have any certainty as to whether death occurred at birth, or subsequently, or in what circumstances. We cannot determine if infanticide, perhaps merely by exposure, was commonly practised. Infants were not viewed as fully human until their soul existed, which according to the Roman writer Pliny was at the age of teething, or perhaps until they were formally recognised by their father. The Lincoln examples were normally placed under eaves or floors, which may in fact itself reflect a kind of re-birth. Two cremations placed in pottery vessels on the rampart of the Park may also have been infants. There was a marked change in attitude towards the burial of infants in the late Roman period, which may reflect the arrival of Christian values – though not widespread Christian belief – affording more respect to the human corpse. Some of the infant burials may have been fourth-century in date, but since there is no inherent indicator of Christian belief, it is not possible to say whether treating them in the same way as other individuals resulted from the influence of Christian values.

Adult burial tends to be more visible in this late period, since ordered inhumation cemeteries were by then more common, and the standard burial practice was that also adopted by Christian communities. The late Roman cemeteries may therefore have contained some Christians, although the evidence that pagan tombs and temples were being demolished in the mid- to late fourth century for re-use in the city wall does not in itself imply that pagan beliefs were in serious decline: they may have merely

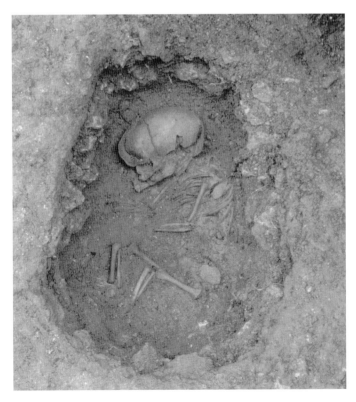

69 *Burial of an infant found adjacent to one of the traders' houses west of the upper city*

117

become mixed with some Christian ideas and practices. The presence of two late Roman burials at St Mark's East may suggest that as the commercial properties were being abandoned, their sites were being used for burial. Subsequently, burials move inside the city walls; this significant phenomenon, dating not before *c.*400, is discussed in the section about the end of the Roman city (chapter 12).

There is much to be learned from studying the population and linking the skeletal evidence to the cultural, but large-scale excavations under controlled conditions are necessary to realise this. These have not yet been possible at Lincoln. The evidence already at our disposal, epigraphic and artefactual, covers only part of the population and thereby produces an unbalanced picture. Yet it is of some interest: the tomb-stones provide some illumination of the social mix, as well as providing evidence for clothing, literacy, longevity, and other aspects (chapter 13). Future studies can benefit from social theory as well as advances in anatomical analysis.

11 Capital: the late Roman period

The administrative and military reforms introduced by the Emperor Diocletian (285-305) at the end of the third century, and built on by Constantine I ('the Great'; 306-337), changed the way in which the Empire was organised and ruled. Britain became a Diocese, one of six in the western empire, and was now divided into four provinces. Following Constantine's Edict of Milan of 313, declaring toleration of Christianity, an administrative system for the Church was established which paralleled the new provincial arrangements, based on the major urban centres. Bishops were appointed to each province; normally they were of aristocratic origin, and in Gaul they became powerful political figures, but we do not have sufficient evidence to tell if this was also true for Britain. The first Christian Council in the west was held at Arles in southern Gaul in 314. The list of those who attended from Britain survives: London and York are mentioned, along with a Bishop Adelphius from 'Colonia Londiniensium', a textual error which must be either Colchester or Lincoln. Since another inscription from Cirencester refers to a provincial governor, it has been argued that the four capitals were at London and York (the two existing), and also at Lincoln and Cirencester. This arrangement would give appropriate geographical coverage of Britain.

Lincoln certainly ranked below York, already a century earlier the capital of *Britannia Inferior*; in the second partition of Britain, the two cities took control of the provinces of *Britannia Secunda* and *Flavia Caesariensis*, with Lincoln now considered as capital of the first. Its boundaries are unknown. The province cannot have extended further north than the Humber, but must have included the modern East Midlands and perhaps more land to the south and west, and conceivably even part of East Anglia. The choice of Lincoln as capital was made partly on geographical grounds, but how far its status as a *colonia* was also a key factor is unknown, in view of Cirencester's apparent (but not proven) selection at the expense of the *colonia* at Gloucester. The decision to promote Lincoln may rather have been related to its economic success, and the fact that it shared a *sevir augustalis* (priest of the cult of the emperor) with York may have contributed.

The exact nature of late Roman towns in Britain is still problematic. The evidence from some other cities could be argued to indicate physical decay from early in the fourth century and significant changes in function. In spite of a decline in building quality, the cities retained sizeable if lower populations and served as centres for administrative, religious and military purposes. There was certainly a reduction in spending on public works in the fourth century, apart from fortifications and, later in the century, a number of churches; but there is also evidence for private wealth and commercial activity. Those public structures which had previously symbolised Roman urban culture – fora, baths, temples – were generally neglected or in certain cases put to different use. Public office and its financial burdens were unpopular. The costs of the army and the maintenance of the administrative and economic system demanded higher taxes, collected through the towns. The government was dependent on the urban network (and vice versa). Trading and manufacturing functions continued, and were in some cases facilitated by the communications systems set up principally for administrative purposes.

Lincoln's newly-acquired capital status, the arrival of government officials with resources and requirements, and the corruption that went with this power, would have benefited the city more than those without an important government function. The needs of the imperial administration demanded a secure base – requiring strong fortifications, comfortable residences, a certain standard of living, and maintenance of communications. The city's functions as a tax collection centre and as a bishopric would have brought further benefits. It might additionally have housed a garrison at times; its administrative importance, strategic location, and strong fortifications would mean that it could have provided an optional stop-over or temporary base. As long as the system was maintained, a measure of prosperity was guaranteed.

Public building

The greatest undertaking for the new government was the strengthening of the fortifications, perhaps both as a symbol of its new capital status and as a deterrent. The city wall was thickened internally or rebuilt, its height now *c*.7-8m, and the surrounding re-cut ditch was considerably wider than previously, at *c*.25m (**70**). In

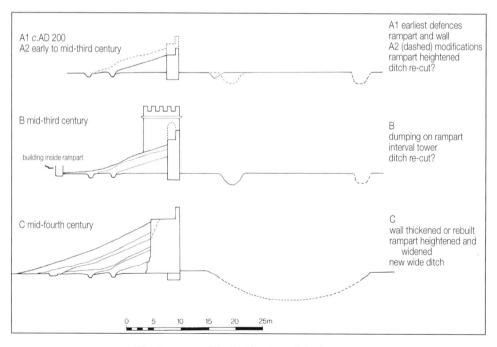

70 *Sequence of the fortifications of the lower city*

71 *Rear of the south tower and thickening of the city wall at the lower west gate*

72 *Reconstruction of the lower west gate and surrounding area.*
D. Vale

places, tombstones and architectural fragments were incorporated into the wall, an unusual phenomenon for Britain. Lincoln also differs from most other major cities in Britain in the absence of external semi-circular towers ('bastions'), except at the third-century gate structures. The style of the later walls is generally conservative; it does not incorporate new ideas, nor even resemble the other late circuits in its province, but rather some late military forts on the northern frontier.

Although the late rampart now extended over the street immediately inside the defences, the street system was largely maintained. At the two new gates in the lower circuit, the lower west gate (**71** & **72**) and the postern opposite the riverfront (**73**), the streets were still being resurfaced at the end of the century. In the east range of the forum, a shop on the main street was used for metal-working and subsequently as a shop where cash transactions were made.

The use of public buildings was, however, in decline. The dating material from the public baths did not provide any evidence to indicate that they were still a vital part of urban social life after *c*.350. We might expect at least one church associated with the bishop, but separate church structures were not a regular occurrence before

73 *The surface of the late Roman postern-gate at Saltergate in the southern defences; note the curving mark made by the gate-post*

the end of the fourth century, nor were they apparently ever very numerous in Britain. Two timber churches were built on the forum courtyard at some date, but in view of the lack of precise dating material it is impossible to establish even if they belong to the Roman occupation, let alone represent the Roman episcopal base. As such, they are discussed in more detail in the next chapter.

The extent to which Christianity penetrated into British society is impossible to define. Early Christian practice in Britain incorporated pagan beliefs and rituals, and the actual display of Christian artefacts could be inspired not so much by belief as social aspiration. It seems reasonable to conclude that there was some acceptance,

74 *Map of the Lincoln area showing late Roman walled sites (squares) and sites which have produced artefacts associated with Christianity (crosses)*

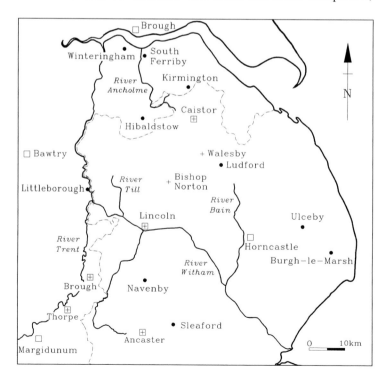

75 *The Walesby lead tank, with a depiction of a baptism*

especially among the intellectual and aristocratic classes, but also retention of old ideas to a greater or lesser extent. While not dominant, evidence for Christian practice is provided, for instance, by the growing number of lead tanks probably associated with baptism – many in the territory of the Bishop of Lincoln (**74**). The bishop may have carried out baptisms by the affusion method (pouring water over the head), as illustrated on the tank from Walesby, *c.*30km north-east of Lincoln (**75**).

As noted in chapter 10, inhumation had by this time completely replaced cremation as the standard burial rite. The change might indicate the influence of near-eastern religions on concepts of the afterlife, with greater respect for bodily remains, but there is little direct evidence of the impact of Christianity on burial traditions. The fourth century is generally characterised by a more orderly arrangement of plots in cemeteries.

A late Roman building at Flaxengate in the lower city was initially interpreted as a church on the basis of the 1976 discovery here of what appeared to be an aisled basilica with an apse, and mortared or tessellated floors. Among the artefacts from the site were some of high status, including exotic glass vessels and marble inlays. Subsequent excavations on adjacent sites have not produced evidence to corroborate a basilican plan, and it may rather have been a domestic structure. This also reduces the likelihood that the remains were those of a governor's assembly or audience hall, but we are largely ignorant of the type of accommodation required by the new provincial administration. Something is known of the mark left by the Imperial Court at Carnuntum (east of Vienna), where its residence in the years AD 171–3 necessitated a large basilican audience hall, and at Aquincum (Hungary), where it resembled a great country house. Scenic views across the river were a feature here, as at Cologne. A huge complex was created at Trier for the imperial presence at what had become the capital of the western empire, including a basilican audience chamber, and there appear to have been linked imperial villas along the valley (the Greetwell Villa springs to mind again). The Roman government was spending huge resources in favoured capitals, at the expense of other urban centres.

The evidence from elsewhere in the Empire suggests that provincial capital status could attract expenditure by the governors, who might also assume control of the civic administration. Space for the provincial government could then have been provided in the civic centre, or alternatively in an entirely new establishment. Continuity of the use of the forum and basilica at Lincoln in the fourth century is clear from the dating material, but as yet there is nothing to indicate the presence of the late Roman government.

Regarding the governor's residence, it is again difficult to find good parallels for what would have been provided, and it is questionable whether expensive new accommodation could be afforded. There is, however, one structure which commands our attention in this respect. The Greetwell Villa (**colour plate 14**) was exceptional for several reasons (p.101): the quality and extent of its mosaic pavements, the palatial scale of its pavilion overlooking the Witham Valley – both back to the city and downstream – and its coin series which runs as late as any from the city. Here lived someone in great, ostentatious splendour till the last few years of the Roman occupation. It is a good candidate for the governor's palace, but it is just as likely that its owner was a wealthy local aristocrat.

Private residences and economic activity

The large residences of the urban aristocracy were at their most sumptuous in the fourth century. The reduced attractiveness of public office meant that investment in private reception areas was a more successful strategy than funding public works. With the exception of the principal street frontages, the hillside was covered largely with houses and their gardens. Their frontages might include a commercial element. Many traders lived behind their shops located on the main routes, for commercial reasons. Most now clustered along the principal roads outside the gates: this was preferable to being hidden away on a back lane inside the walls, but some traders in such locations were apparently thriving and still expanding in the fourth century. Noxious industrial activity tended to take place in fringe areas, normally on the edge of the conurbation. Pottery production did not significantly change from that of the later third century until the last decade or so. It is apparent that there was an increasing dependence on local Swanpool products throughout the period. There is some indication of abandonment at the fringes by the middle of the fourth century, but most establishments seem to have survived into the 360s-70s, if not beyond.

More dumping took place at several sites on low-lying ground, as well as on the waterside, with the construction in places of a new vertical timber revetment. It was probably linked to a significant rise in the river level, but it is as yet not clear if this rise was caused by a hydrological engineering project or was simply a natural phenomenon. In either case, it must represent a political decision to invest in future security and prosperity. On the riverfront immediately south of the walled city, there was wholesale dumping on a scale which can only have been organised by the authorities. The material of which the dumps consisted included vast quantities of discarded bones of large mammals from butchers' waste, to serve as hardcore, and it also contained traces of grain pests indicating nearby heated buildings (p.110-12). Dumps of fourth-century butchers' waste were also found on the back of the rampart and elsewhere.

12 The end of Roman Lincoln

The city in transition

The processes whereby the Roman city declined to the point of almost complete abandonment by the mid-fifth century, and what if anything survived in the way of organisation and population, are only now beginning to be understood. It was at the mercy of a number of factors beyond the citizens' control, although the extent to which climate, disease, or internal political problems were decisive has been exaggerated by some writers. Certainly, an inexorable transformation was well under way by the time of the Anglo-Saxon invasions. The termination of coin supply, as part of Britain's exclusion from the imperial economic and taxation system at the beginning of the fifth century, meant that an urban community was no longer sustainable.

One symptom of the decline was that archaeological evidence for the period becomes much less substantial than previously. Dating evidence is less abundant after c.380, and the few historical references cannot be taken at face value. One of the problems is determining precise dates for the abandonment of buildings, in other words, their final occupation deposits – not that we would expect all these deposits to have survived subsequent disturbance. Occupation may have continued through several structural phases after that of the latest datable artefact. The pattern of wear on surfaces may be a clue.

There is plenty of material evidence to suggest occupation at Lincoln in the last decades of the fourth century. The coins and pottery confirm that the walled city and the suburbs were still occupied but that some sites were being deserted in the mid- to late fourth century. Several buildings were demolished, while others were rebuilt. The number of coins found (that is, lost and not recovered) suggests a 'high point' in the 360-70s, later than many other towns. The sharp drop which followed might indicate a serious contraction of the money economy from c.375. Most of the coins of the very late fourth century or the beginning of the fifth came from two sites on the hillside, from the nearby riverside, and from the Greetwell Villa. The distribution does, however, suggest continuing commercial activity, and comfort for a few.

At the same time, there are signs of a more basic material provision for many. For instance, a trader's house in the southern suburb was reduced in scale: its new back wall was built much closer to the street. Some streets were abandoned, others were resurfaced: the latest documented is that at the Lower West Gate, still being maintained as late as c.400, yet at the same time dumping of rubbish was taking place adjacent to the nearby city wall. An evocative picture is presented by the gradual decay of the interval tower on the western defences at West Parade, in particular the evidence of the animal bones. Here, a location visited regularly by owls, dead dogs were dumped, an activity also found at Silchester and considered to have involved a ritual element – but these activities cannot be dated closely and possibly began earlier in the century.

To summarise the chronicle of physical decay, almost all of the sites occupied in the third century were still vibrant in the early to mid-fourth century, but less than half of them may have continued beyond *c.*370-80. The fringes of the suburbs were more vulnerable to the drop in activity, but otherwise the latest occupation (*c.*375-410) occurs across the city as a whole. There are clear signs of occupation inside the upper city, including the forum, at residential sites in the Lower City demonstrably occupied at the end of the century, and activity at the Waterside. The latest structures were of poorer build-quality than previously, involving a reversion to dry stone walls or timber-frame construction, possibly linked to the end of the stone-building industry. The reduction in scale and quality of the trader's house at St Mark's Church probably reflects the drop in commercial activity; at the same time continuing settlement is discernible at several nearby plots – traders who attempted to soldier on regardless. Some extra-mural processes were re-located inside the walls: evidence for lead-smelting, iron-working, and other metallurgical processes suggests a significant change. The changes in economic activity could reflect a serious disruption in the Roman supply system from *c.*370-80, resulting in a greater reliance on available materials, a scenario which would help explain the increase in metal-working. As a whole, the evidence might be taken to indicate a different type of settlement, still urban but with a smaller population, many living in timber buildings, and practising industrial processes and perhaps also agriculture and horticulture within the walls.

The last category of activity may be suggested by deposits of the so-called 'Dark Earth' which overlie the latest identifiable Roman occupation at Lincoln (and in several other cities), but its interpretation is still problematic and apparently more complex. The current favoured explanations include soil formed as a result of biological re-working of late Roman deposits, over buildings and in waste ground used for subsequent rubbish disposal, or material derived from middens or from manure, with stock kept in nearby animal pens. At Lincoln, Dark Earth has been identified at several sites in the lower city and in the southern suburb. It is clear that some occurrences were dumps of material laid deliberately. In certain cases material may have been placed between the ruins of stone walls to create level ground for new timber buildings or horticultural activities. On the other hand, the fresh condition of the pottery, and the absence of any impact by roots on animal bones, argue against the idea that it represents cultivation. The date of the Dark Earth deposits is uncertain but appears in many cases to belong to the last generation of the Roman occupation, *c.*380-410. It implies continuing occupation of an urban nature, but also signals the demise of large-scale town residences, and their replacement – if at all – by an architectural style of modest timber shacks. With the interruption in and subsequent ending of coin supply, there was an inevitable collapse in pottery and other manufacturing production.

In the period from AD 406, as political and military problems mounted, the sudden burst of precious hoards in Britain demonstrates that many of the most wealthy families were in flight. In Lincoln, one of the latest sites to remain in occupation, judging from the late coin series, was the Greetwell Villa site. This would be consistent with its having been the base of the governor.

In spite of the problems surrounding them, the imperial officials and civic administration may have endeavoured to keep the system working, perhaps based in the forum. If the bishop had a church, here or elsewhere, this might have been another focus for part of the surviving community. After *c.*410, and the official Roman withdrawal, a community of urban scale was simply not sustainable, but some of the population may have remained.

A thread of continuity?

In spite of the appointment of the bishop, Christian worship may have been restricted to private houses until a site could be found for a new building in which the congregation could meet, and generally this did not happen before the late fourth century, even in Gaul. The evidence for fourth- or fifth-century churches in Britain is slight and even some of these are not universally accepted.

The sequence of two successive timber churches in the forum courtyard at Lincoln has been briefly mentioned above. Their western ends were outside the area of excavation, but presumably were formed by the west portico of the forum (**76 & 77**). They measured respectively *c.*15m and *c.*25m in length: the second structure could have held at least a hundred worshippers. There were clear similarities in construction methods. Both had chancel screens based on 'post-in-trench construction'; the earlier chancel was very short and square-ended, its successor roughly semi-circular (**78**).

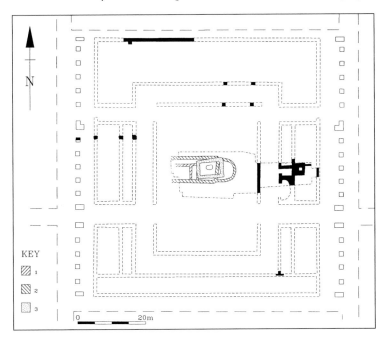

76 Plan of the earliest churches in the forum (site of St Paul in the Bail); the third church in the sequence was definitely Anglo-Saxon in date, and probably a chapel containing an important grave

77 *Reconstruction by David Vale of the second church in the sequence; note the relationship to the portico of the forum*

78 *The eastern end of the second church showing its apsidal chancel and the line of the chancel screen indicated by post-holes*

Burials only began to penetrate within the walls of Roman towns from the end of the fourth century, linked to the cult of saints, and their relics, but even in Rome few burials can be dated as early as the fifth century. Radiocarbon dating of the earliest graves at St Paul-in-the-Bail, including some graves which had been cut into the wall-line of the second church (and therefore post-dated its demolition), favours a late Roman, or sub-Roman (i.e. fifth- or sixth-century) context. The dates would have to be stretched to accommodate an early seventh-century context, although the original interpretation of the apsidal church was as one that belonged to the Anglo-Saxon conversion in AD 627-8: Bede recounts that a 'stone church of remarkable workmanship' was built by Bishop Paulinus, who had converted the royal represen-tative, Blecca, and his household. The general range of the radiocarbon dates would rather suggest that the demolition of the second building took place before that episode. What may have been a foundation deposit (of relics?) from a feature imme-diately west of the second church's screen, i.e. beneath the altar, gave a medial date of AD 441, that is, likely to be fourth- to sixth-century. The only other clue is a coin of Arcadius of *c*.390 from the forum surface, and this is of uncertain stratigraphic significance in relation to the church buildings.

Their plans do not allow further precision: good parallels for both are found across the western empire from the late fourth century to the seventh century. The context for their construction is therefore subject to different interpretations. There are, moreover, few close parallels for churches in the courtyards of fora – most occur in the Mediterranean region, but there is a possible British example at Exeter, where sub-Roman burials were found adjacent to the civic basilica, and a church may have lain nearby. More churches were actually formed out of elements of public baths, perhaps related to the nearby presence of water to facilitate baptism: the well in the forum at Lincoln may therefore have been the crucial factor in choosing the church's location.

St Paul was a popular dedication in the last few decades of the fourth century. If a Roman date is accepted, the central location would suggest that it was part of the bishop's establishment, perhaps forming one element in an 'Episcopal Group' consisting of two churches (one of which might be used for relics or other purposes), a baptistery – the well in the east range – and accommodation nearby. It is possible that the civic basilica was converted to the other of the churches. The centre of the forum would have been a prestigious and appropriate position, given Lincoln's provincial capital status, and the church a new symbol of authority. It might, perhaps, have continued to function under the bishop for several decades after the withdrawal of official Roman support in AD 410. There were continuing contacts between British and Gallic bishops, which reinforced a Roman identity. An alternative construction date in the fifth or sixth centuries is, however, just as likely for these two churches and is more consistent with the radiocarbon dates. Even then, a bishop might still have been involved as a senior aide to the leader of a community wishing to promote the idea that he was the true heir of the Empire.

Of course, the early cathedral may have lain elsewhere in the city, wherever more space was or was made available – perhaps as a gift by a local aristocrat, a phenom-

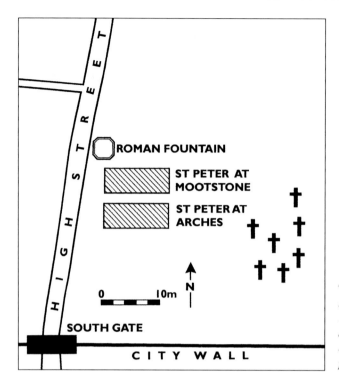

79 Plan of the possible arrangement of early churches at St Peter at Arches in the lower city, suggesting a double church and a baptistery reusing the public fountain

enon well-documented on the continent. One site which was a significant ecclesiastical focus in the early medieval period, St Peter at Arches inside the south gate of the lower city, may have owed its location to the surviving public fountain, a convenient structure for re-use as a baptistery; but there is no evidence that the church here was built before the seventh or eighth centuries (**79**).

The almost complete absence of early Anglo-Saxon finds from the city reinforces this idea. The exceptions are individual pots from the Greetwell Villa, and from the flue of one of the Swanpool kilns. The significance of these is uncertain: were they deposited deliberately by the incoming rulers, as a symbol of their assuming control? The fifth century is almost completely silent in terms of evidence, but that does not mean that nothing was happening in the town. Whoever took control had the benefit of a fortified site of symbolic value, good communication routes, and some impressive surviving buildings. Much of the rest of the city meanwhile was in decay, gradually reverting to waste ground. The forum-basilica at Lincoln might have continued under new rulers as a political and ecclesiastical focus. For the mass of people, whether those few still within the town walls or in rural settlements, we may be sure that a subsistence lifestyle was all that was on offer. The urban centre of the Roman period, with its easy access to social amenities and plentiful material comforts, was no longer.

13 City life: culture, economy and society

The Roman urban settlement at Lincoln survived for over 300 years and, as has been described, during that period it changed and developed in various ways. The chronological and topographical aspects of that development are covered in previous chapters, but there are certain themes which deserve special treatment: they include the culture, lifestyle and beliefs of its inhabitants; what we know of the economy of the city; its population (not just the few individuals documented) and the nature of its society. The extent to which Roman Lincoln was essentially Roman in the metropolitan sense, or rather Roman provincial, is one which can be simply answered. 'Roman' culture was not pure Roman even in Italy; there were regional variations. To what extent, then, was Lincoln representative of the north-west Provinces (Britain, northern Gaul and northern Germany), rather than merely a Romano-British sort of place, or was its culture akin to other *coloniae* rather than tribal capitals, or to that of the Roman army, or to the native Britons? In some ways, and at different times, it reveals elements of all of these. The present chapter draws together the evidence for these themes, and where appropriate, repeats some of the evidence already discussed in previous chapters.

The native British and Roman military contributions

As a background to the Roman settlement, a few words are in order on the existing native occupants. There is no doubt that the leaders of the tribes of south-east Britain had extensive contacts with the Roman world before the Claudian conquest. These contacts took the form not just of trade and the importation of wine and other luxuries from the Mediterranean, but also through sending the sons of the aristocratic elite to Rome. The lasting impression such visits made, and the training in the Latin language, encouraged the adoption of Roman ways of defining status and power. Although it was on the periphery of the south-east region, and did not benefit from such close contact, the Corieltauvi tribe did, like the other tribes, produce its own coinage, derived from Gallo-Belgic types. The existence of a currency made trade with the south-east and mainland Europe possible. The availability of iron as well as salt, and of food from pasture, the sea, and rivers, meant that the tribal leaders of the Corieltauvi had access to considerable wealth. As we have seen (chapter 2), wealth was partly expressed in the later Bronze and Iron Ages in the form of votive offerings into water. An increase in material culture and a growth in the size of the settlements are the most obvious characteristics of the last century of the pre-Roman Iron Age, although we still do not have sufficient evidence to understand the exact nature of the settlement which existed in the Lincoln area.

The Roman legionary occupation, closely followed by the settlement of veterans, imposed new physical forms on the areas north and south of the river. The local population may not initially have welcomed the Roman presence, but the arrival of the army did provide some opportunities, the range of which increased after the *colonia* was founded: there must have been a native element, as well as immigrant traders, in the settlement from the start. The life of the city reflected these various elements.

The early decades of the colony were probably dominated by the several hundred ex-legionaries, many of southern European origin (although fewer Italians than the earlier colony at Colchester) who brought with them a military and a continental culture (**colour plate 2**). The influence of this imported culture may have been dominant for a generation or two, reinforced by the city's status and the development of Roman imperial architecture. In time, as the descendants of the first colonists began to see themselves as Romano-Britons rather than Mediterraneans or ex-soldiers, and there was more influence from other natives, immigrant traders, and craftsmen, the city would have come to resemble the other cities of the province. In examining the architecture and town planning of the city, and its art, economy and diet, we can recognise influences from the military, from other cities (both from the Mediterranean and from the north-west provinces of the Empire), as well as native elements, sometimes coalescing. These aspects are considered in turn.

Planning and architecture

Roman architecture was new to Britain: it was also a useful if expensive vehicle for making a political statement, for government and local officials alike. Public works constituted the major element in the early development of the city, as it did in the twentieth-century British mindset in its perception of the Roman occupation: we have generally been impressed by the considerable engineering achievements and comfortable with the classical idiom of monumental architecture, exemplified by the portico in both public and private buildings. Our attitudes have been shaped to some extent by the British Empire. Moreover, the strength of Roman construction has meant that the evidence for the symbols of Roman power has survived well, to the detriment of both other types of structure and settlement, and of other aspects of life (discussed below). Yet it is still true that the evidence for Roman architecture in Britain is poorer than other provinces, and that Lincoln, in spite of easy access to good building stone, has not so far produced as much material as might be expected. The reasons for this are probably connected with its subsequent history – a long period of neglect in a harsh climate, and incorporation of much that remained into medieval buildings.

The differing construction methods of the well-built streets of the city have been described in previous chapters. The main north-south route (*cardo*) at least, and possibly the principal east-west street (*decumanus*), were paved through the upper city and on the steeper part of the hillside. Other routes were capped by 'softer' surfaces of pebbles or gravel, sometimes mixed with crushed stones and sand, appearing to be mortared from the way the materials bonded. The material required for both may have become more easily available once the local quarries were working fully. Covered drains were a common feature in the upper city; on the hillside, in spite of side-drains, heavy rain produced drainage problems.

The rigorous planning of the upper city, based on that of the fortress, with its principal monument at the junction of the two main streets, was a common feature of early colonies going back four centuries. The main route through the town was also that which ran back to and therefore symbolically linked the city to Rome. The central building in the early colonies was normally a state temple containing a statue of the emperor, often with a forum, a gathering place for rituals and festivals, attached. The evidence from Lincoln is consistent with this picture. Later, the sign of a successful city was a full range of public amenities, with less significance attached merely to the forum-temple: certainly many of the tribal capitals of Roman Britain belong to the second group. In Lincoln's case, the rebuilt forum was still an impressive complex, and its status as a *colonia* was still a mark of loyalty to the empire.

The lower city was distinguished by the more pragmatic layout of the hillside, and both parts of the walled city in turn contrasted with the suburban roadside expansion. There was deliberate zonation, updated to take account of changing circumstances, and allowing for open spaces. The split-level character of the city, with power and prestige based on the hilltop, commerce and industry in the valley, and a varying mix including wealthy residents in between, was echoed in the medieval topography. Certain features, such as gates and façades of public buildings, provided impressive approaches, and the long haul up the hill gave a sense of anticipation as well as requiring some physical effort, as visitors experience today.

Although the early *coloniae* were normally graced by a temple of the imperial cult as a priority, the decision as to which public works were actually built was largely left to the local community. Apart from the administrative and other functions which took place in the forum, other structures were provided for religious and social rituals, and for the performance of cultural works and spectacles. What evidence we have for Britain suggests that the major projects – sometimes lasting decades – were undertaken at the expense of the authorities; only temples seem to have been provided largely by private benefactions. Those who undertook this burden did so as part of the price paid for seeking and maintaining their local status and popularity, in order to achieve election to the highest offices. There was also scope for those of lower rank, even ex-slaves, to rise up the social scale by sponsoring public buildings – notably the *sevir augustalis* who rebuilt a temple in return for his election to the priesthood.

Our knowledge of the fortifications, both walls and gates, is good. For the remaining public monuments of *Lindum Colonia*, however, even the forum and public baths, there is much still to be learned. It is clear from surviving fragments that several others fronted the principal two streets. The most important buildings were at the centre of the city, the highest point. Some indication of the appearance of the main structures is provided by both their layout and by evidence for their structural components and decoration. This included decorated antefixes for gable ends and roof finials, both for special buildings. Triple or double courses of bonding tiles were a distinctive characteristic, possibly enhanced by 'false' decorative techniques such as pointing and incising, as well as painting of moulded stones, and marble veneers. The general impression given by the best architectural material from Britain – and Lincoln was no exception – is that its decorative source was provided by sculptors from north-east Gaul (*Gallia Belgica*) and cities along the Rhine rather than further afield (**80**). The same was true of non-architectural sculpture. There are links in terms of architectural decoration both with cities in the south-east part of Britain, and with some towns and fortresses on the edge of the military zone, including Chester and Wroxeter. The pattern suggests that immigrant sculptors were moving around the province. Many buildings had decorated walls and ceilings, and tessellated floors, all designed to be appreciated as an ensemble. The evidence for wall-painting is not abundant nor outstanding in quality; most fragments indicate panelled decoration. Some better quality work survived, but only in small fragments, such as that including floral designs from the early forum (**colour plate 18**), the house later covered by the rampart on Silver Street (**colour plate 13**), and the plant forms radiating from roundels from the fourth-century Greetwell Villa (**colour plate 8**). Mosaic pavements have fared little better, but there are some later figured scenes from the upper city. The Lincoln pavements show affinities with both those from further south, in the heart of Corieltauvian territory, and some from the Humber region: again, itinerant craftsmen are suggested. The outstanding example is the Greetwell Villa, with its long corridor of 'reticulated' *tesserae* (with serrated edges) considered to be the work of imported craftsmen, perhaps from Italy (**colour plates 12 & 14**).

80 *Decorated cornice fragment from a temple or funerary monument re-used in the lower west gate*

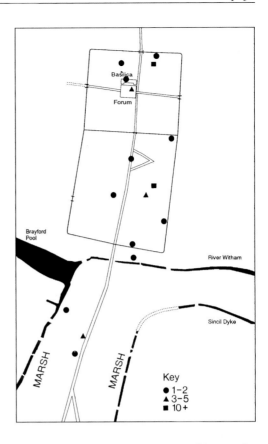

81 *Distribution of Roman wall-veneers; the earlier are from public buildings in the upper city, the later from private houses*

By the later Roman period, the expenditure previously devoted to public works had shifted partly to fortification, the *sine qua non* of a late Roman city of any standing, but principally to private investment in aristocratic residences, rural as well as urban. The distribution pattern of window glass and imported marble veneers echoes this shift (**81**). In the second century, most fragments were associated with the public baths and the forum. Later they came from the elite residences on the hillside, and a few examples were even found in the traders' houses in the southern suburbs. The types of housing plan were all imported, from the long strip-buildings of traders to more ambitious examples with courtyards. Although some residences were extensive – that found at Spring Hill had at least twelve rooms (**49**) – the larger houses were not of the most sumptuous Mediterranean type, but were, like many in Britain, influenced partly by military buildings and some Gallic types. They may often have consisted of a range of rooms leading on to a corridor, with an extra wing added to form an L-shape, their Mediterranean credentials reinforced by the common use of porticoes. The earliest houses were built in timber, but could still have some sophisticated internal appointments: only a small sample has yet been investigated and on the whole such detail has been poorly preserved. There does appear to be a discernible chronological development from timber-framed to full stone construction, reflecting to some extent the increased investment in houses from the mid- to late second century. Mosaic pavements and painted walls and ceilings were especially characteristic of the fourth century, the great epoch of private ostentation, and some residences also had a piped water supply (**50**). Several of those excavated at Lincoln included some open space, or gardens, in their plots. The motivation behind expenditure on lavish schemes was partly socio-political, to provide spaces in which to impress visitors and do business in the Roman manner. Rooms might also be let for commercial activity. Most will have belonged to a number of powerful families – perhaps 20 to 30 – who were prominent in public life, although eclipsed by the new bureaucracy in the fourth century.

Art and society

Other insights into the culture of the city are provided by evidence for the use of various artistic forms. The best of the sculpture found at Lincoln – the charioteer (**colour plate 26**), the figure of *Fortuna* (possibly representing the image, or guardian spirit, of the city; **colour plate 28**), and the boy with a hare (**colour plate 27**) – are, as noted, clearly the work of sculptors from the Rhineland. However, there also appears to have been a workshop at Lincoln producing good work in the local limestone. It is not appropriate to judge its quality on purely Greco-Roman criteria, for the native British eye was more adjusted to a 'Celtic' perspective, which gave prominence to linear pattern. Among its products are the mother-goddesses and the relief sculpture of Cupid and Psyche (**colour plate 11**), implying some familiarity with the myths of Greco-Roman culture and a Latin education.

Art was used for a number of other functions, as well as satisfying acquisitive and aesthetic desires, and for political and often for religious purposes (see below), for commemorating the dead, and for images of the emperor and the gods. It took several forms, in various materials, and in particular the Roman period in Britain witnessed an explosion in the production of small statuettes. The best known of these from the Lincoln area is the bronze figure of Mars found in the Fossdyke canal, sponsored by two brothers and competently made by Celatus, a bronze-worker possibly based in the city (**colour plate 29**). Other objects, including a pottery vessel decorated with a flying phallus, possibly made for amusement, remind us how Roman artistic taste and perceptions differed from our own. The wide range of artefacts found provides an idea of the material available in such quantity, for the first time in British history, to those who could afford it.

Economy

The Roman system facilitated this growth in materialism through investment, expertise, and trade. The need to develop first the fortress then the town created a boom in building and a demand for materials, skills, and labour. The initial concentration on timber shifted from the early second century into stone public buildings and the city walls. Most building materials could be provided locally; others, like the

Pennine sandstone used for the forum colonnade, had to be brought some distance, as did Purbeck stone from Dorset, while real marble veneers formed an element of the trade in luxuries from the eastern Mediterranean. The costs were high, but so was the motivation to impress.

Stone was easily accessible on the ridge, and lime was also needed for mortar and wall-plaster. Tiles, in their various forms, could also be produced in the locality (**50**): some from Lincoln were stamped, to identify the batch as well as by the workshop. They mainly consist of the basic forms for roofs and hypocausts, but included the rare antefixes for decorative gable ends. Tile was an important constituent of *opus signinum*, a type of cement used for floors and linings, including the jacket for the aqueduct pipe (**56**). Slate is also found, and could be obtained from the Jurassic Ridge. Gravel and sand for mortars and roads were also to hand in the valley, but the vast amounts of timber required must have involved some organisation of transport, and woodland management. These mineral sources and extractive industries were probably owned and organised by the government. The suburbs and the industrial zones at the edge of the city must have been very busy at times.

The pattern of coin loss in Lincoln is largely consistent with that of other Roman cities in Britain, including the tribal capitals. From the number of coins lost (and since found), it seems likely that, by the mid-third century at the latest, transactions were carried out using cash. The mass of goods available for purchase in the city must reflect that cash economy, partly stimulated by private enterprise but perhaps under civic organisation for some commodities, such as the meat supply (see below). It is also possible that the local government controlled the supply of other goods. Since we cannot really understand how the economy worked – statistical information is too limited – we have to rely on a number of possible indicators, which may be misleading rather than representative.

One of the most widely-used indicators is pottery, since such large amounts have been found and studied. There is again a mix of local production, and imports from other sources in Britain and some abroad. These last include large containers for foodstuffs, *amphorae*, which some consider to have been secondary to the movement of wool and more basic foodstuffs and taking advantage of existing supply-routes to add on luxuries: perishables may be a more accurate indicator of trading patterns. At least the sources of the imported vessels do provide a clue to some aspects of trade (**82**). The *amphorae* found at Lincoln, bringing products such as wine, olive oil, olives, dates, honey and fish sauce, were produced at several different sites around the Mediterranean. The samian industries of Gaul provided fine table wares until their demise in the third century (**colour plate 20**). The pottery assemblage from the city as a whole resembles that of the other major urban centres of Roman Britain. For instance, some of the fine wares of the second century were supplied from the Nene Valley, and the *mortaria* (mixing bowls) of the third to fourth centuries were dominated by the Mancetter–Hartshill kilns of Warwickshire, until being finally overtaken by the local Swanpool industry in the later part of the fourth century.

Earlier, although potters had moved to Britain from the Rhineland, some of the legion's requirements, notably for cooking pots, were supplied by native potters. The

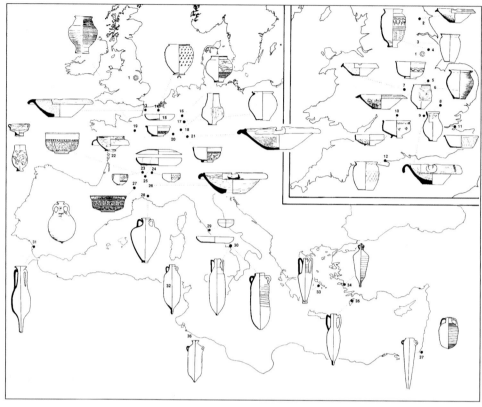

82 *Sources of Roman pottery found at Lincoln:*
Britain: 1. Lincoln; 2. Crambeck; 3. South Yorkshire/North Lincolnshire; 4. Market Rasen;
5. Peterborough; 6. South Midlands; 7. Mancetter/Hartshill; 8. Much Hadham;
9. St Albans/Verulamium; 10. Oxford; 11. North Kent Marshes; 12. Wareham/Poole.
Europe: 13. Pas de Calais; 14. Braives; 15. Gallo-Belgic; 16. Cologne; 17. Mayen; 18. Trier;
19. North Gaul; 20. Montans; 21. Soller; 22. Poitiers Region; 23. St Remy en Rollat/Vichy;
24. Lyons; 25. Lezoux/Les Martres de Veyre; 26. Rhone Valley; 27. La Graufesenque/South
Gaul; 28. Lower Rhone Valley; 29. Cosa; 30. Campania; 31. Baetica; 32. Tunisia;
33. The Aegean; 34. Western Asia Minor; 35. Rhodes; 36. Tripolitania; 37. Egypt

location of known kilns from the late first century shows considerable movement around the edge and surroundings of the city, from North Hykeham to the South Carlton and Racecourse areas, and the suburb close to the lower east gate (**58**). The last of these concentrated on mortaria, others on copies of the black-burnished pottery found over much of Roman Britain. From the evidence for distribution of their products, it appears that these local industries won commissions for supplying the army in the north, but more work is needed on kiln sites and on the range of products and their distribution.

The local ceramic industry later found a more settled, semi-rural locus in the Boultham/Swanpool area. This location may have been chosen on the grounds of accessibility to fuel rather than clay, or it may have provided both together. Sand and gravel for mortar and roads were available in the same area, and iron-working may also have been carried out nearby: an industrial complex, perhaps. By this later period, the city was more self-sufficient, and there were few imports, but the Swanpool products may not have penetrated far beyond Lincoln's immediate sphere of economic influence: concentrations of kilns are known to have existed in the Trent Valley and in the Market Rasen area, only 25km away (**60**).

Pots were used principally for kitchen or table functions, some for both. Others were essentially storage vessels, while some miniatures served for votive purposes. Closer dating and sourcing are facilitated by the makers' stamps on some mortaria and samian vessels (**colour plate 20**). Some vessels had painted legends making their function clear – e.g. *bibe* ('drink me!') – and graffiti add to our knowledge of literacy and attitudes. A fragment of an *amphora* from the fourth-century rampart-dumps at The Park, by the Lower West Gate, has a painted inscription which appears to read 'salted olives', and possibly gives their source as Picenum in Italy (**colour plate 17**). Other *amphorae* came from as far away as Baetica, in southern Spain (these were particularly common), North Africa, and the eastern Mediterranean.

Imports to Lincoln from the Roman Empire are found from the time of the legionary occupation, with much then and later from southern Gaul, both table wares and wine *amphorae*. Within the range of samian table-ware from Gaul, Margaret Darling has suggested that the use of decorated forms was an expression of status. A decorated bowl would cost a day's pay for a soldier, about twice that of a plain form. During the second century, the industries of central Gaul replaced southern Gaul as the primary producer, and decorated wares were a less significant element of their repertoire. Against the background of that trend, it was apparent that the commercial traders of the suburbs were buying less decorated vessels than the higher-status inhabitants of the walled city.

A range of exotic foodstuffs is suggested by the different *amphora* types, most dating to before AD 150. That the wine trade continued well into the third century, although fewer Mediterranean *amphorae* occur by that time, seems to be confirmed by the Bordeaux altar of AD 237 set up by the Lincoln/York official Marcus Aurelius Lunaris (**colour plate 10**). Olive oil (or fish sauce) *amphorae* from North Africa were still being imported in the late third century, and have on the whole been found at the aristocratic houses in the lower city. Most fish sauce actually came from southern Spain.

Some other individual pots identified by Margaret Darling deserve special mention. One of these is a beaker stamped by the pottery Camaro, possibly based in Braives, in Belgium. It was globular in form, decorated with 'bobbles' and coated in mica gilt. From excavations in 1959-62 on the south tower of the upper east gate came fragments of a large beaker with 'barbotine' decoration, i.e. wet clay squeezed on to the body of the pot. The subject of the decoration has been identified as one of the labours of Hercules, that of capturing the Ceryneian Hind. Hercules is depicted as wielding his club while kneeling on the hind and gripping its antlers. The function of this vessel is uncertain; its size and form suggest that it was static, and might have served as an element in a personal shrine, or simply for decoration.

Other materials

The evidence for glass vessels from Lincoln reflects the changing emphasis of their use in Roman Britain: in the legionary period, bottles and bowls predominate, while later it was jugs and cups. No evidence has yet been found for a glass manufacturer in the city, but this remains a possibility. Glass and metal vessels were optional and more expensive alternatives to pottery, but changing patterns of relative use may rather have followed fashion. Colourless drinking vessels became a more common form in the later second century, and some were decorated with trailing. More ambitious versions featuring bird and flower snake-thread motifs were produced in the eastern Mediterranean. One special type of container was the unguent bottle, used for carrying oils and perfumes (**colour plate 7**): some were found together with cremations for anointing the corpse with oils. The latest Roman material included bowls, and claw- and conical-beakers of high quality, particularly from the aristocratic residences. In 2001, a very fine globular beaker with an elaborate decorated neck turned up in a pit close to the waterside west of the city, together with a late Roman bronze hanging bowl, both presumably buried for safe keeping at a time of increasing uncertainty – or perhaps as part of a ritual – but never recovered.

Another major industry, stimulated initially by the army's demands, and found in all Romano-British towns (as well as rural locations), was iron-working. Sources of the ore were not too distant and the activity appears to have taken place in several establishments in the suburbs. Although the site of the anvil could not be detected, the presence of a smithy was distinguished by the slag or by tiny fragments of hammer-scale scattered around when the hot metal was hammered. The finds of 'Smith-god pots' from the trader's house at St Marks were another sign. This site also produced part of a portable tile oven vessel (*clibanus*). Some smelting furnaces have also been found; this activity may have taken place in the backyards. A wide variety of iron products was manufactured, and some have survived. One of the shops in the forum fronting on to the main street was used at various times for iron-working, silver-working and copper-working. The latest Roman levels at Hungate contained large quantities of slag suggesting that a smithy now formed part of the establishment here, possibly working on a government contract. Coal, not uncommon in Roman Britain, was used as fuel for several of the smithies. It is clear from finds of bone and antler objects that these too were being made in the city. The rubbish dumps at The Park (Lower West Gate) and the Waterside sites were particularly prolific.

Lifestyle

Other metal artefacts found in households included the kitchen utensils – metal cutlery and skillets – and lighting implements – such as oil lamps and candlesticks (candle fat was less expensive than oil). Some families could afford luxury items such as a bronze wine-pourer. Small-scale domestic industry is suggested by the presence of needles, spindle whorls, querns (millstones) including some imported lava types, and baking ovens. The clothing and food industries at which these finds hint are poorly represented in the archaeological record, since only at a limited number of sites has the evidence survived for organic materials. There are, for instance, no fragments of textiles as yet from the Roman deposits in Lincoln, but since these two aspects of consumption are highly fashionable in modern society we might expect that there will be an upsurge in research into them. What we know of clothing suggests that the normal garb for 'Romanised' individuals consisted of the unbelted 'Gallic cloak', which was a wide tunic. Capes, fastened at the neck, were a necessary adjunct in cold weather; women adopted a rectangular cloak. For aristocrats, clothes could be used for displaying status, but the toga was probably only seen on the top officials and at formal occasions. Figured tombstones, which normally depict individuals as they or their family wish them to be remembered, provide images of clothing and of changing fashions in hairstyles; there are few from Lincoln – notably that of the councillor's wife Volusia Faustina (**24**). Footwear, and the off-cuts from its manufacture, have appeared in some quantity with the investigation of waterlogged deposits: the vast majority of the seventy or so Roman shoes came from the Waterside North sites (**colour plate 21**). They have yet to be analysed in detail, but one almost complete example from the St Marks area was of the type known as a '*carbatina*'. The greatest quantity of material that was worn, however, consists of fittings and jewellery – brooches and other fasteners, bracelets, necklace beads, strapends, pins, rings (for both ears and fingers) and gems – in various metals, glass, bone, jet and shale, and other stones (**83**, **colour plate 22**, **23** & **24**). There are also items associated with personal care – mirrors and manicure tools, and hairpins.

Evidence for diet occurs principally in the form of animal and fish bones, shells, and preserved plant remains. There is some evidence to suggest that the Roman army influenced the diet of Britain generally, with a heavily increased demand for beef: this pattern was also found in the urban centres. Britain appears to fall generally into the dietary pattern of the north-west provinces, along with northern Gaul and Germany, eating more beef than the people of the Mediterranean, while Britain consumed more lamb than her continental neighbours. Certainly, there is good evidence from Lincoln that smoked and cured shoulders of beef were popular in both the early and late Roman periods. Cattle, sheep, and pig were all consumed in some quantity, with both cheap and more expensive cuts available, together with fish (some local, some imported), oysters from the coast, certain types of fowl and game, and a

83 *Jet pin from the lower west gate site*

range of cereals, fruit and vegetables. In general, there is no apparent distinction between the colonies and the tribal capitals, although this may not have been the case until the last of the legionary veterans and their influence had disappeared.

The Roman impact, which is discernible before the conquest in the south-east, was to extend the range of foodstuffs available, largely but not exclusively in terms of fruit and vegetables, and particularly at the luxury end of the market. Some plants were introduced which were suited to the British climate. The sample recovered from Waterside North in 1988 included a few cereal grains, figs, flavourings including coriander, beet, and dill; these must represent only a small proportion of what was available. To the food must be added both native beer and imported (and later British) wine, some for religious use.

Clues to how the area surrounding the town was organised for food production are provided by archaeological features and the evidence for animal bones and plants. Remains of horticulture or agriculture were identified at Chaplin Street, to the rear of the commercial buildings on the street frontage in the southern suburb. They may have formed part of an area of urban allotments as was discovered outside the west gate at Colchester. The supply of meat was related to some extent to dairy, wool and leather production, and the fact that the cattle whose bones were found were not juvenile stock suggests that they had previously served as traction and dairy animals, some based on villa estates. In contrast, a good proportion of the sheep was too young to have been used for wool production. Pigs were probably reared within or adjacent to the city, while cattle and sheep may only have been brought in for butchery, perhaps after slaughter and skinning on the edge of town. Larger stock seems to have been introduced in the later Roman period, and it was only then that improvements in agricultural equipment became apparent.

A large area many miles square was required to feed the city's population of several thousand with cereals, meat, fruit and vegetables, but the extent of this 'hinterland' will have varied in size during the Roman occupation. It was located as close to the city as other priorities and constraints – such as industrial zones – allowed.

Religion and belief

Ritual was a part of everyday life in the city, and took various forms, in line with the diverse range of religious beliefs and activities. These are only partly represented in the archaeological record by temples, altars, sculptures, statuettes and figurines, and the physical survivals reflect practice rather than actual belief. There were regular festivals, some involving the sacrifice of an animal at an altar and a subsequent meal. Of course, the official state religion and the classical Roman deities were a significant element in civic life, but the Roman government was generally tolerant of existing religions. Thus there is plenty of evidence for native deities – both the Romans and the Britons were polytheistic – and sometimes the 'Celtic' gods were actually linked to the imperial cult: the inscription from nearby Nettleham commemorating an arch dedicated both to the 'divine emperors' and to *Mars Rigonemetos* ('Mars, King of the

Sacred Grove') is a good case in point (**61**). The Roman god Mars was identified with a native cult: this 'syncretism', or *interpretatio romana*, was common practice where native and Roman gods shared similar characteristics, but we do not fully understand how the relationship of the two was perceived by the population. It cannot be assumed that the Roman deity was seen as dominant.

The Roman impact on native religion included the introduction of a new architecture for the public cults, which were intended to impress the population. The *coloniae* were ideal vehicles for promoting the new imperial identity, and a temple to the cult of the emperor would be its focus. The early forum at Lincoln may have incorporated that temple: certainly the finding of the base of an equestrian statue and the bronze foreleg of a horse strongly suggest an association with the imperial image. The cult was supported by a panel of priests, some of them successful traders or ex-slaves: at Lincoln they include M. Aurelius Lunaris who dedicated the Bordeaux altar, and the anonymous freedman who sponsored a rebuilding of the temple in the area of the forum.

Temples to the Roman gods Mercury and Apollo are evidenced by inscriptions set up by their worshippers. The former stood adjacent to Ermine Street in the lower city, while that to Apollo may also have been on the hillside: the inscription had been built into the later city wall, as had altars to Mars and to 'the fates and the spirits of the emperors'. The last of these, still visible inside St Swithin's Church, was dedicated by G. Antistius Frontinus, the treasurer of a burial club, a guild set up to ensure adequate funds for members' burials. Other types of deity imported included the 'spirit of the place' – *genius loci* – inscribed on an altar found on the east side of the city: the inscription refers to the fulfilling of a vow, a common element in Roman ritual.

The distribution of altars and of Romano-Celtic temples in Britain shows that the former were favoured by the army, and as such were largely to be found in the north and west, while the temples were confined almost exclusively to the urbanised south-east of Britain. The fact that Lincoln had both may not merely reflect military influence from its origins as a colony for legionary veterans, nor that it was close to the boundary between the military and civilian regions. Perhaps, like London, it was a cosmopolitan city with sufficient amenities to be visited regularly by the military. Two separate sculptures of the three 'mother-goddesses' have been found in the city, as well as at Ancaster and other towns; their origins may be connected with the movement of people (perhaps ex-soldiers) from the lower Rhine (**84**). Some of the oriental religions that found their way to Britain are also linked to military influence; and in some cases as exclusive cults made attractive by their mystification. Mithraism was one of these – although its values were actually more in line with those of the Romans than the eastern Provinces. A suggestion has been made that the sculpted stone in the tower of St Peter at Gowts Church, at the southern limit of the southern suburb, initially represented a Mithraic figure. The bronze head of the Egyptian god Atys was another oriental import.

As well as sculptures, small objects and statuettes became commonplace in Roman Britain, many based in domestic shrines. Examples from the city include the smith-god pots possibly set up at a smith's shrine together with other objects,

84 *Fragment of relief sculpture of mother-goddesses from west of the lower city*

including a face pot and a phallic pot. Other face pots have been found, all considered to have had a religious purpose. The phallus was sometimes used as a sign for good luck, or to ward off bad luck – representations on the city wall at East Bight were presumably for this purpose. The figure of the *dea nutrix* (nursing goddess) from traders' houses west of the upper city, where infant burials were also found, was connected in some way with fertility (**85**). These pipe-clay figurines were made in Gaul. The relief sculpture of Cupid and Psyche from the house at Hungate suggests some familiarity with the Roman myth, but may rather have been an amusing conversation piece of which the owner was proud.

The evidence for burial can also be interpreted, but not without some caution, to indicate beliefs about the after world. The only cemetery in the city to have been investigated under modern controlled conditions was the small area of the legionary burial ground at Monson Street, which was not limited to the soldiers' graves. Here, the actual burial practice took a Roman form, but some of the offerings may reflect native practice. The nature of graves as a whole, including some exotic tombs, inscribed tombstones (more common in the legionary period), and round barrows – is again very much in the Roman mould, with parallels in north-east Gaul.

The impact of Christianity on this pattern is uncertain, but the Lincoln area has produced plenty of material evidence for baptism in rural communities (**74**). The new practice might have been expected to make the deepest impact in the city itself, yet pagan beliefs certainly persisted here – as confirmed by the votive offerings of chicken bones made in constructing the late Roman gate at The Park. Christianity was not formally the official religion of the empire or pagan temples closed until the late fourth century. Both systems may have survived the Roman period, together with native 'Celtic' religion, and soon further complicated by Anglo-Saxon importations.

Population and society

The population, which during the legionary period probably numbered in excess of 5,000, and dropped for a while, may never have risen to more than 10-12,000. Based on the extent of its occupied area, Lincoln was not one of the largest cities of Roman Britain – it was in the second rank with the other *coloniae*. The population itself was as mixed as the diverse religions. Military or ex-military personnel, immigrant merchants and traders, both native and immigrant craftsmen, government officials, and rural natives were all present at various times in varying proportions. Just a very small proportion are identifiable as individuals from inscribed tombstones – the Greek Flavius Helius (perhaps a trader, teacher or doctor), the Gaul Sacer (possibly another trader) from the Senonian tribe (the area around the modern town of Sens), and the apparent nonagenarian Claudia Crysis are some of the more memorable individuals documented. That there was geographical and social mobility is clear: people moved around, even to or from other provinces, and some succeeded in raising their status. Potters and some other craftsmen – the bronze worker Celatus springs to mind – are identifiable from their stamps; these craftsmen were generally low on the social scale. There were wide discrepancies between rich and poor, with wealth based on ownership of land, such that the elite had all the power until the advent of the military-administrative bureaucracy in the fourth century. They were the group that, along with the military, had closest contact with the Latin language and Roman culture, but to survive as a 'top' family was financially difficult and eventually too great a burden to sustain.

The stature of the people of Roman Britain was a little shorter than today, but not significantly so. We have little evidence from the city on longevity; those whose

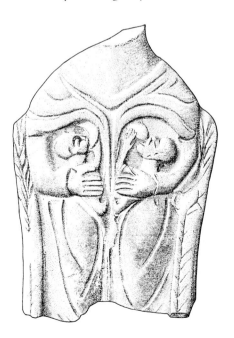

85 *Clay-pipe figurine of* dea nutrix *(nursing goddess) from a trader's house in the suburb outside the upper west gate*

age at death is noted on their tombstones died at a wide variety of ages and include children, young and very elderly women, and soldiers of early middle age. The provincial picture suggests that most people suffered from physical ailments linked to their work, from tooth decay, and from various infections, and died by the age of 50, but some lived much longer: whether we can believe that Claudia Crysis was actually 90 years old when she died is another matter. Epidemics and poor harvests could have a significant effect. Many died young of illness and many infants were stillborn or subject to deliberate neglect or exposure. Doctors were more likely to be on hand in the cities, but their effectiveness was limited.

We can only try to understand what it was like to live in the past through our own experiences. Modern urban society – especially that of the metropolis, but also to some extent in smaller cities – is a special type of society, living a purely urban lifestyle. This may have been the case with the great centres of the Roman world, but was only partly true of cities like Lincoln – the vast majority of Roman Britain's population lived and worked in the countryside and only visited the towns occasionally. But for those who had a major stake in the political and economic life, there was a vital and visible role to be played, and the official rituals and festivals helped to emphasise their dominant position. The physical fabric which they helped to create itself had an impact on town dwellers and visitors alike – particularly the principal monuments, but also the streetscape and buildings, peopled by a range of individuals and animals, and marked by commodities for sale, amenities available, wheeled and water-based traffic, sounds, and smells, and lighting. To rural peasants, it may have been both bewildering and exciting. The urban environment varied, as today, from impressive monuments displaying exotic decoration, to unsightly rubbish dumps and neglected areas of weeds with their quota of pests; from temples for sublime worship to stinking urinals, and drains, and dung-laden streets; and from large mansions with striking reception areas, to the packed and graffiti-ridden districts of the urban poor, and the noxious, grimy and smoky industries on the edge of town. In all, therefore, life in Roman Lincoln displayed many of the facets of its modern counterpart – but without the huge advances in technology and the resultant speed of change, scale of operation, and domination of mechanised traffic.

This review has, in conclusion, suggested that there were significant military and some native influences from the start, and that the presence of the imperial image was an essential element of the early city. Later, Lincoln settled down to be one of the more successful cities of Roman Britain in economic terms, and its culture became more akin to that of the other cities, with access to selected Mediterranean luxuries, but otherwise that of Britain itself within the wider sphere of the north-west provinces. As we saw in the previous two chapters, capital status in the fourth century brought both renewed continental influences, and the more self-sufficient but still buoyant economy which characterised Britain until the final decades. It was the persisting image of empire, rather than any economic prospects, which gave it an opportunity to survive at all beyond the political end of Roman Britain.

14 Where to see Roman Lincoln

The geographical situation of Lincoln, in the Witham Gap, is best appreciated from the higher part of South Common, or on the north side from a number of vantage points in the Cathedral area – notably the garden of the Medieval Bishop's Palace, or the Observatory Tower of Lincoln Castle. This last elevation also permits views down the Witham Valley, as well as to the south and south-west along the Roman routes, and along part of the Fossdyke canal to the west. On a clear day, the gap can also be seen from the A57 to the west and from the A158 Horncastle Road many miles to the east.

A tour of the visible remains in the city should take in the following sites, numbered as on the map (**86**). These mainly consist of the remains of the city wall and gates, plus some other major buildings.

1   East Gate: North Tower and adjacent city wall in the forecourt of the Lincoln Hotel (formerly The Eastgate Hotel). Plans are in place to improve the condition and interpretation of this monument.

2   (optional): wall to rear of the Lincoln Hotel (via the carpark to the north): an impressive sketch of the core of the rebuilt wall, surviving here to its highest point above its base (*c*.2m below the modern ground level).

3   Walk northwards along East Bight, past the different brick of the hotel's meeting room, where an interval-tower and later thickening were uncovered in 1971.

4   Continue northwards and then westwards along East Bight until you reach a surviving fragment of the city wall. This is part of the later rebuilding (fourth-century), and has survived presumably because it stood adjacent to the water tank (*castellum aquae*) which stored water from the aqueduct and distributed it to the nearby baths, only *c*.50m to the south, and other sites supplied. The outline of the tank is marked in the ground, and there is a notice board at the site.

5   To the west of the property boundary and beyond to the north, but still in a rear garden of a house on Church Lane, is part of the early city wall and an added second-century internal tower (not accessible to the public). Some impression can be obtained of the width of the late Roman ditch.

6   At the end of East Bight, beyond a fragment of the late thickening of the wall in the garden of Newport Cottage, is the Newport Arch, the inner face of the north gate in its third-century form (with medieval additions and modifications to the north). This is one of the surviving jewels of Roman Britain, as the only

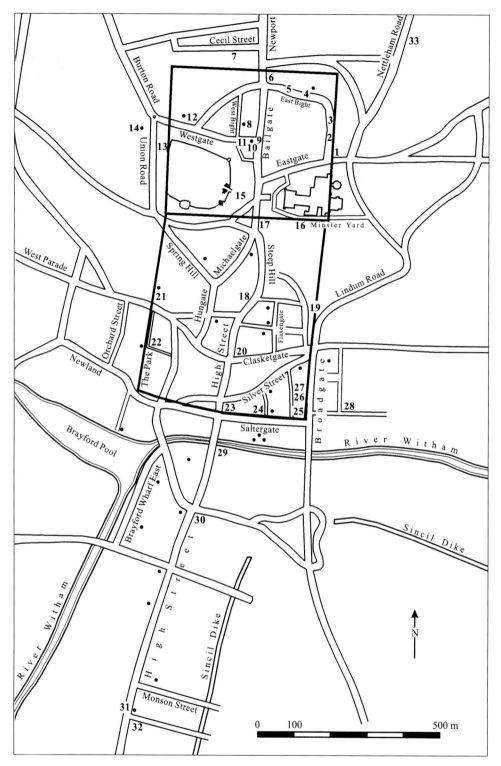

86 *Map showing main excavation sites mentioned in the text, and those where remains are visible*

gate-arch still used by traffic – but not without its hazards (**5**). On the north side (across Bailgate), the lower, chamfered base of the front of the west gate-tower can be seen, and the blocked lower part of the western side passage, which help to indicate the Roman ground level and the extent to which the gate-arches have been filled.

7   If you have plenty of time, proceed a little to the north and then left into Cecil Street. In less than 100m, go through the arch of Mary Sookias House on the left (south) side, where a stretch of the city wall exposed in the late 1970s can be seen. Little of the facing survives, but some putlog holes for scaffolding are still visible. There is an interpretation panel. (This section may be re-covered in the next few years to protect it.)

8   Return back to Newport Arch and turn right into Chapel Lane – a diagonal post-Roman street ignoring the Roman grid, but linking the Roman north and west gates – and turn left into the narrow passage known as West Bight. Towards the southern end is the so-called Mint Wall, the north wall of the Roman town hall (*basilica*). An interpretation panel explains the remains.

9   Return to West Bight and turn left, coming in a short while to the street of Westgate and, on its south side, the site of St Paul-in-the-Bail. Go immediately eastwards (left) to Bailgate, where you will note circular granite-setts on the surface of the street. These denote the positions of a row of 19 columns which formed the frontage of the forum. The most northerly columns still stand *c.*1m high in the cellar of 29 Bailgate (private, and not currently accessible; a door marks the location and the date of discovery).

10   Return to the site of St Paul-in-the-Bail. Towards its eastern end, fragments of some walls of the forum's east range, and the head of a well are exposed (recently capped in turf). These were excavated in 1979, but have deteriorated from weathering, and the 'soft-capping' has been laid to arrest the decay pending long-term proposals. The interpretation panels and planting scheme at the site are also to be improved at the time of writing.

11   The main garden area surrounds the site of the long sequence of churches possibly beginning as early as the fourth century AD (chapter 12). The plan of the second church in the sequence is marked on the ground, and there is an interpretation panel at the west end.

12   From here walk westwards along Westgate, on the north side of the Castle. The original discovery of the defences of the legionary fortress was made in the garden of Westgate Junior School in the 1940s.

13   At the end of Westgate, turn left into Union Road, and immediately south of 'The Victoria' public house, you will see the Norman west gate of Lincoln Castle. It was in the castle bank immediately to the north of the Norman gate that the Roman west gate was revealed in 1836 (see cover).

14 Across Union Road, you may enter the grounds of the former Lawn hospital, now a visitor and conference centre. On the ground floor of the separate building (Charlotte House) is the Lincoln Archaeology Centre, which explains, using hands-on techniques, some of the processes involved in urban archaeology in Lincoln. It is open daily, and entrance is free of charge, but the Centre's long-term future is in doubt pending the opening of the new City and County Museum (see number 19, below).

15 Out of The Lawn grounds, turn right (southwards) along Union Road, then turn left at the end and continue in that direction along Drury Lane until you reach Castle Hill (a square), where you may wish to admire the view and visit other attractions.

16 One of these attractions is the medieval Bishop's Palace, accessible from the south side of Minster Yard (English Heritage; entrance charge). The interpretation of this monument has been much improved in 2002. The east wall of the site, beyond the East Hall, has some masonry of the Roman city wall in its lowest courses: those that follow the slope. At the south-east corner of the site (actually within the grounds of the Usher Gallery) a fragment of the core of the Roman city wall is visible. It will have to be conserved in the near future. The garden of the Palace provides a good location from which to view the Witham gap and the lower part of the city.

17 Return to Castle Hill, and turn left into the aptly named Steep Hill. At number 44, you can enter the shop on the east (left-hand) side, part of the outer wall of the eastern carriageway and of the *spina* of the south gate were exposed in 2001 for the first time in almost 300 years. Their discovery confirmed that this gate had a double carriageway, the western arch having been on the line of Steep Hill itself.

From this point, the rest of the visible remains are more widely spaced, and to venture down to the bottom of Steep Hill means also that you will have to find your way back up again. Fortunately, there is now the option of an uphill-downhill bus link which leaves regularly from the pedestrian precinct north of the Stonebow.

18 If you do wish to continue, go down Steep Hill. This is a medieval deviation from the paved Roman route, which ascended the steepest part of the slope in a series of monumental steps and ramps. Vehicles meanwhile took a circuitous route: a diagonal street surfaced in pebbles and with traces of wheel ruts was found adjacent to St Martin's Street. By the twelfth-century Jews House is Jews Court, the offices of the Society for Lincolnshire History and Archaeology, which include a well-stocked bookshop on all aspects of the county's history and archaeology.

19 Opposite here is Danes Terrace, at the end of which the Usher Gallery is visible, where the coin collection is displayed. The adjacent site across Danesgate is due to become the new home of the City and County Museum from the spring of

2005. A selection of artefacts from Roman Lincoln will be on display, and the Museum will provide an introduction to the material in other ways.

20 Returning along Danes Terrace to the line of Steep Hill and The Strait, you eventually come to the top of High Street, which here overlies Ermine Street. On the east side immediately before the traffic lights is a night club in a basement which also contains the flue of a Roman hypocaust system thought to be part of a public baths establishment (**3**). It was one of the public monuments on the Ermine Street in the lower city: a temple and public fountain lay to the south.

21 At the traffic lights, turn right along Corporation Street and West Parade until you come to the line of a steep cobbled path called Motherby Hill, after the police headquarters. The path lies roughly on the line of the west wall of the lower city, and a small, unimpressive fragment of wall is displayed together with an adjacent explanatory panel.

22 Cross West Parade and go down the street called 'The Park' towards the large brutalist concrete building which houses the offices of the City Council (as well as the County's Sites and Monuments Record). On your right is an impressive stretch of city wall (fourth-century) and the bases of the towers of a contemporary gate. The north tower incorporates some re-used decorated and moulded stones, now somewhat damaged by exposure and human agency. Conservation work and improvements are planned. The finest piece, a decorated cornice, has been re-located to the foyer of City Hall and has been replaced by a fibreglass replica. There is an interpretation panel.

23 Continue southwards to Newland and then east along the pedestrianised Guildhall Street as far as the Stonebow arches on your left. This lies over the south gate of the lower city, whose plan is not known.

24 Further along to the east, along Saltergate, the basement of the Royal Bank of Scotland, entered at the junction with Bank Street, contains a section of the south wall and a postern gate (excavated in 1973-4) which led to the riverside. The basement is, however, only open on selected days (contact the City and County Museum Offices on 01522 530401 for details).

25 Further along Saltergate is the impressive Victorian church of St Swithin which currently houses, at its west end, a Roman altar to the fates set up by the treasurer of a Roman burial club.

26 Immediately to the north of St Swithin's Church, the thirteenth-century Greyfriars currently serves in place of the Museum and normally has archaeological exhibitions (free entrance). It is likely to close for such purposes when the new Museum is complete.

27 Also here, entered from Free School Lane, is the Central Library, a good base for research, since its local history collections are well-resourced.

28 Across Broadgate, on St Rumbold Street can be found a similar haven, the Lincolnshire Archives Office (membership required, but no charge for joining). To its rear are the current offices, store, and Conservation Laboratory of the City and County Museum. These can be visited by *bona fide* students for research purposes.

29 Returning to the Stonebow, you can proceed down High Street over the twelfth-century High Bridge which sits on the site of its Roman predecessor. Allow for the fact that the Roman river was much wider. In fact, it almost lapped up against the city wall, before the waterfront was advanced later in the Roman period.

30 Just beyond the end of the pedestrian precinct, and adjacent to the railway crossing, is the church of St Mary-le-Wigford. Its Saxo-Norman tower, added to an earlier, narrow nave, displays the founder's dedication, re-using a Roman tombstone of a Gaul named Sacer.

31 A few hundred metres down High Street brings you past Monson Street (where legionary tombstones were found) to Sibthorp Street. On its north side, the twelfth-century St Mary's Guildhall (currently the offices of the Lincoln Civic Trust) was built over the eastern part of the Roman Fosse Way, part of which is exposed under a glass floor. The base of the first Roman milestone south from the city, found during conservation works in the early 1980s, rests here. The building is not normally open to the public.

32 High up in the tower of the nearby St Peter at Gowts Church is a sculptured stone which, it has been suggested, depicts the Mithraic god Arimanius, re-used to represent Christ in majesty.

33 The only other physical fragment to see is part of the Roman aqueduct pipe, which is displayed in the foyer of the Safeway supermarket towards the end of Nettleham Road, close to where is was excavated (a mile or so from the city centre). To the north of the store is the spring known as the Roaring Meg which traditionally (but probably incorrectly) has been identified as its source.

Several items from Lincoln are on display in the Roman Britain Gallery at the British Museum, and many others are in store.

Guide to further reading

The *Lincoln Archaeological Research Assessment* (edited by David Stocker, with M.J. Jones and Alan Vince), which will be published by Oxbow Books in conjunction with English Heritage and the City of Lincoln Council in 2003, contains a more detailed account of the origins and development of the city, including the Roman period, than can be presented here. It will be fully referenced, and the reader is therefore recommended to consult it for the sources of much of the information presented in this book.

The *Assessment* is partly derived from the Lincoln Urban Archaeology Database (UAD), also compiled with guidance and grant-aid from English Heritage. It is hoped that it can be made available to the public in revised, digital form in the not too distant future. The Database in turn was created from the information already available in the files of the Lincoln City and County Museum, the Lincolnshire Sites and Monuments Record, and an archive of records and various publications resulting from excavations in the city.

The principal accounts of excavations from 1970 appeared in the series, *The Archaeology of Lincoln*, published by the Council for British Archaeology in 14 separate fascicules between 1977 and 1999. They included reports on Roman coins, fortifications (separate monographs on the upper and lower cities, the second including artefacts), and pottery. More recently, there is a new series, *Lincoln Archaeological Studies*. Its first two volumes were *Pre-Viking Lindsey* (edited by Alan Vince, 1993), and *Of Butchers and Breeds* (on vertebrate remains; by Keith Dobney *et al.*, 1996). The rest of the series will consist of volumes of excavation reports on the Wigford/Brayford Pool area (by Kate Steane *et al.*, published 2001), the Upper City (also by Kate Steane *et al.*, to be published late 2002), and the Lower City (in preparation); and corpora of pottery (by Margaret Darling and Barbara Precious) and glass (by Jennifer Price *et al.*). The *Assessment* will represent the culmination of this period of analysis and of the series. Specialist archive reports will be accessible through the City and County Museum.

This book and the UAA also largely supersede previous articles on the Roman city, the most recent being two contained in H.R. Hurst (ed.), *The Coloniae of Roman Britain* (Journal of Roman Archaeology Supplement Series no. 36, 1999). Other essential syntheses of note include those by Ian Richmond, in *The Archaeological Journal* (vol. 103; 1946); by Ben Whitwell, in *Roman Lincolnshire* (1970; new edition 1992); and by John Wacher in the two editions of *The Towns of Roman Britain* (1975; revised edition 1995).

General introductions to Roman Britain abound. An historical approach is dominant in two standard works: *Britannia: a history of Roman Britain*, by S.S. Frere (3rd edition, Routledge, 1987), and *Roman Britain* (volume II in *The Oxford History of Britain*, 1981), by Peter Salway. The same author's *Oxford Illustrated History of Roman Britain* (1993) is more approachable and up to date. These must be set against Martin Millett's *The Romanisation of Britain* (Cambridge, 1990), and *Roman Britain* (Batsford/English Heritage, 1995), which emphasise the contribution made by the native aristocracy.

153

There are several other books of great merit. *The Blackwell Companion to Roman Britain*, edited by Malcolm Todd (forthcoming, 2003) will form an authoritative reference work; it contains essays by various specialists. The Tempus list also contains several works on various aspects, some of them listed below.

In the chapter-by-chapter lists below, the works cited largely exclude those to be found in the detailed bibliography of the UAA, and are accordingly limited to a few essential books, apart from chapters 1, 2, and 11, which have no equivalent in the ARA.

Chapter 1: Roman Lincoln lost and found

Chandler, J., 1998, *John Leland's Itinerary: Travels in Tudor England*, Stroud
Drury, M., *c.*1880, *Notes on the excavations for sewer works at Lincoln*, Lincoln Central Library
Eaton, T., 2001, *Plundering the Past: Roman Stonework in Medieval Britain*, Tempus
Everson, P.L., 1980, 'Thomas 'Governor' Pownall and the Roman Villa at Glentworth, Lincolnshire', *Lincolnshire History Archaeology*, 15, 9-14
Finley, M.I., 1985, *Ancient History: Evidence and Models*, London
Gascoigne, J., 1994, *Joseph Banks and The English Enlightenment*, Cambridge
Hunt, R.W., 1965, 'William Pownall: Antiquarian', *Annual Reports and Papers of the Lincolnshire Architectural and Archaeological Society*, 9.2, 158-63
Piggott, S., 1976, *Ruins in a Landscape: Essays in Antiquarianism*, Edinburgh
Piggott, S., 1985, *William Stukeley*, Thames and Hudson, London
Schnapp, A., 1996, *The Discovery of The Past: The Origins of Archaeology*, British Museum Publications, London

Chapter 2: Prologue

May, J., 1976, *Prehistoric Lincolnshire (History of Lincolnshire, Vol. 1)*, Lincoln
Straw, A., 2002, 'Lincolnshire – gaps and more gaps', *Geology Today*, 18, 1-19
Swinnerton, H.H., 1937, 'The Problem of the Lincoln Gap', *Transactions of the Lincolnshire Naturalists' Union*, 145-53
Ussher, W.A.E., Jukes-Brown, A.J., & Straham, A., 1888, *The Geology of the Country Around Lincoln*, Memoirs of the Geological Survey
Waller, M., 1994, *Fenland Project No. 9: Flandrian Environmental Change in Fenland*. East Anglian Archaeology No. 70, Cambridge
Wilkinson, T.J., 1987, 'Palaeoenvironments in the Upper Witham Fen', *Fenland Research*, 4, 52-6

On ritual aspects of deposition:
Bradley, R., 1998, *The Passage of Arms* (2nd edition), Oxbow Books, Oxford
Pryor, F.M., 2001, *Seahenge: New Discoveries in Prehistoric Britain*, Harper Collins, London

For the Witham Valley, see three forthcoming papers by the same two authors:
Stocker, D., & Everson, P., 'The Straight and Narrow Way: Fenland Causeways and the Conversion of the Landscape in the Witham Valley, Lincolnshire' in M.O.H. Carver (ed.), *The Cross Goes North: An Archaeology of Conversion*; Boydell & Brewer
'The Landscape Context of the Causeways of the Witham Valley' in D. Start & S. Catney, *Time and Tide: A Research Agenda for the Witham Valley* (Heritage Trust of Lincolnshire), *The Landscape of Barlings Abbey* (monograph)

On the late Iron Age:
Creighton, J., 2000, *Coinage and Power in Late Iron Age Britain*, Cambridge
Cunliffe, B.W., 1991, *Iron Age Communities in Britain* (3rd edition), Routledge
Gwilt, A., & Haselgrove, C.C. (eds), 1997, *Reconstructing Iron Age Societies*, Oxford: Oxbow Monographs 71 (see in particular the article by S. Willis on the East Midlands)
May, J., 1996, *Dragonby: Report on Excavations at an Iron Age and Romano-British Settlement in North Lincolnshire*, Oxbow Books, Oxford

Chapters 3-5: Roman military occupation

On the invasion:
Manley, J.F., 2002, *AD 43: The Roman Invasion of Britain: a reassessment*, Tempus
Frere, S.S., & Fulford, M.G., 2001, 'The Roman Invasion of AD 43', *Britannia 32*, 45-55
On the ancient British landscape and settlement:
Roberts, B.K., & Wrathmell, S., 2000, *An Atlas of Rural Settlement in England*, English Heritage, London

On Roman forts and fortresses:
Bidwell, P.T., 1997, *Roman Forts in Britain*, Batsford/English Heritage, London
Brewer, R.J. (ed.), 2000, *Roman Fortresses and their Legions*, Society of Antiquaries of London/National Museum Gallery Wales (includes an article by L. Keppie on the Ninth Legion)
Johnson, A., 1983, *Roman Forts of the First and Second Centuries AD in Britain and the German Provinces* A. & C. Black, London

On aspects of construction:
Shirley, E., 2001, *Building a Roman Legionary Fortress*, Tempus

On roads:
Davies, H., 2002, *Roads in Roman Britain*, Tempus

Chapter 6: Colony
Hurst, H.R. (ed.), 1999 *The Coloniae of Roman Britain: New Studies and a Review*, Journal of Roman Archaeology Supplement, No. 36

On the population:
Birley, A.R., 1979, *The People of Roman Britain*, Batsford, London

On building methods:
Adam, J.-P., 1994, *Roman Building: Materials and Techniques*, Batsford, London

On the range and design of buildings:
de la Bédoyère, G., 2001, *The Buildings of Roman Britain*, Tempus

On architecture and decoration:
Blagg, T.F.C., 2002, *Roman Architectural Ornament in Britain*, British Archaeological Reports, British Series, 329
Gros, P., 1996, *L'Architecture Romaine: I, Les Monuments Publics*, Paris

Chapter 7: Planned growth

On housing:
Perring, D., 2002, *The Roman House in Britain*, Routledge, London

On sculpture:
Huskinson, J., 1994, *Corpus of Sculpture in the Roman World: Roman Sculpture from Eastern England*, British Academy, London

Chapters 8-10: Expansion beyond the walls
Esmonde Cleary, A.S., 1987, *Extra-Mural Areas of Romano-British Towns*, British Archaeological Reports, British Series, 169

On the aqueduct and related aspects:
Jones, M.J., forthcoming, 'Sources of Effluence: Water through Roman Lincoln', in P.R. Wilson (ed.), *The Archaeology of Roman Towns*, Oxbow Books, Oxford

On 'small towns':
Brown, A.E. (ed.), 1995, *Roman Small Towns in Eastern England and Beyond*, Oxbow Books, Oxford
Burnham, B., & Wacher, J.S., 1990, *The Small Towns of Roman Britain*, Batsford

On the mosaics from the Greetwell Villa (and other sites in the city):
Neal, D.S., & Cosh, S.R., 2002, *Roman Mosaics in Britain, Vol. 1: Northern Britain*, London: Illuminata for the Society of Antiquaries of London

On the Lincoln waterfront:
Steane, K., *et al.*, 2001, *The Archaeology of Wigford and the Brayford Pool*, Lincoln Archaeological Studies, Vol. 2, Oxbow Books, Oxford

On burial and cemeteries:
Pearce, J., Millett, M., & Struck, M. (eds), 2000, *Burial, Society and Context in the Roman World*, Oxbow Books, Oxford
Philpott, R., 1991, *Burial Practices in Roman Britain: A Survey of Grave Treatment and Furnishing, AD 43-410*, British Archaeological Reports, British Series, 219

Chapters 11-12: The late Roman Period; The end of Roman Lincoln

Esmonde Cleary, A.S., 1989, *The Ending of Roman Britain*, Batsford, London (reissued 2001, Routledge)

The imperial background to the fourth and early fifth centuries is set out in the new edition of the Cambridge Ancient History, Volume XIII, *The Late Empire, AD 337-425* (1998), edited by Averil Cameron and Peter Garnsey. It includes essays on government by Christopher Kelly, and on the cities by Bryan Ward-Perkins.

Much else has been written on this period in Britain and abroad in recent years, among which are three books published by Tempus which take different viewpoints:
Dark, K., 2000, *Britain and the End of the Roman Empire*
de la Bédoyère, G., 1999, *The Golden Age of Roman Britain*
Faulkner, N., 2000, *The Decline and Fall of Roman Britain*
There are several papers on this period in *Pre-Viking Lindsey* (p.153)

Chapter 13: City life

For the late Iron Age period, see references for chapter 2 above.
For structural aspects, see references for chapters 6-8 above.

Croom, A.T., 2000, *Roman Clothing and Fashion*, Tempus (this is partly based on two fundamental articles by J.P. Wild, published in volumes only available in academic libraries)
Fentress, E. (ed.), 2000, *Romanization and the City*, Journal of Roman Archaeology, Supplementary Series, 38 (in particular, articles by H.R. Hurst and P. Zanker)
Henig, M., 1995, *Art in Roman Britain*, Batsford, London
King, A.C., 1999, *Diet in the Roman World: a regional inter-site comparison of the mammal bones*, Journal of Roman Archaeology, 12, 168-202
Price, J., & Cottam, S., 1998, *Romano-British glass vessels: a handbook*, Council for British Archaeology, York

Chapter 14: Where to see Roman Lincoln

A separate leaflet is being published shortly. A similar account to that given here can be found in the standard guidebook to Roman Britain:
Wilson, R.J.A., 2002, *A Guide to the Roman Remains in Britain*, (4th edition) Constable, London

Glossary

antefix decorative, triangular ceramic tile positioned over the eaves or at the gable-end of a roof

alluvium material deposited by a river

amphora large pottery container, used for transporting wine, olive oil, etc.

apse a semi-circular room or recess

basilica large hall, sometimes aisled; a form used for town halls and churches

canabae officially-let traders' buildings (literally 'booths'), outside the fortress gates

cardo (*maximus*) principal street of the Roman city, linking two of the gates; in Lincoln's case, running north-south (cf. *decumanus*)

cognomen third name, or surname (plural: *cognomina*)

colluvium deposit created by hill-wash

colonia highest status awarded to provincial cities, with full Roman citizenship; sometimes settlements of legionary veterans

cornice one of the architectural elements above the colonnade

cornucopia horn of plenty, signifying abundance, fertility, good harvest

decumanus (*maximus*) the second main street of a Roman city, linking two of the gates

decurio member of the town-council (*ordo*)

diatoms single-celled algae, ecologically sensitive

epigraphic refers to writings on objects, e.g. inscribed tombstones and dedications

exedra a recess, usually semi-circular or rectangular, within a building to house a small room

extra-mural situated outside the city walls

forum open space in civic centre

hypocaust underfloor heating-system, allowing warm air to be circulated

ludus amphitheatre-like enclosed area used for military training

mortarium pottery mixing bowl

oppidum name for a town; usually confined to large native centres rather than Roman cities

opus signinum	waterproof cement or concrete, made out of mortar containing crushed tile; used for floors and tank-linings
ordo	town council, of up to 100 decurions
porta decumana	back gate of the fortress, to the rear of the *principia*
porta praetoria	front gate of the fortress, leading along the *via praetoria* to the *principia*
porta principalis	one of the two main side gates of the fortress, linked by the *via principalis*
postern	minor gate
praetentura	that part of the fortress in front of the *via principalis*, the main street running along the front of the *principia* (literally, the 'forward tents', from the time when the army was in temporary accommodation)
praetorium	the legionary commander's residence, to the side of the *principia*
prata legionis	land outside the fortress used for accommodating the legion's requirements for grazing, etc. (literally, the 'meadows of the legion')
principia	legionary headquarters building at the centre of the fortress
revetment	support for earth bank in timber, turf, or stone
RIB	*The Roman Inscriptions of Britain, Volume I* (by R.G. Collingwood & R.P. Wright, Oxford, 1965)
samian ware	fine pottery, mainly tableware, covered in a red gloss; made in Gaul and exported widely throughout the Roman Empire until the early third century
sevir augustalis	one of the panel of priests in each city responsible for maintaining the cult of the emperor
spina	the central wall, or 'spine', between two arches
territorium	the land around and formally belonging to the city; individual plots were owned by citizens of the colony
tessera	fragment of 'tessellated' pavement or mosaic
vexillation	a detachment, perhaps two or more cohorts (each of 480 men) of a legion
via praetoria	the street in the fortress running from the front gate (*porta praetoria*) to the *principia*
via principalis	main street of the fortress running between two of the gates and meeting the *via praetoria* at the entrance to the *principia*
vicus	civil settlement outside the fortress (not the same as the *canabae*); later, a ward, or district, of the city
voussoir	wedge-shaped stone forming part of an arch

Index